Self-Sufficiency
Foraging for Wild Foods

Self-Sufficiency
Foraging for Wild Foods

David Squire

**lifestyle
books**

Read. Learn. Do What You Love.

Published 2016—IMM Lifestyle Books
www.IMMLifestyleBooks.com

IMM Lifestyle Books are distributed in the UK by Grantham Book Service,
Trent Road, Grantham, Lincolnshire, NG31 7XQ.

In North America, IMM Lifestyle Books are distributed by Fox Chapel Publishing,
1970 Broad Street, East Petersburg, PA 17520, www.FoxChapelPublishing.com.

ISBN   978 1 5048 0034 1

10 9 8 7 6 5 4 3 2

Printed in Singapore

The author and publishers have made every effort to ensure that all information
given in this book is safe and accurate, but they cannot accept liability for any
resulting injury or loss or damage to either property or person,
whether direct or consequential or however arising.

CONTENTS

INTRODUCTION

It is impossible to know exactly when our ancestors became foragers but it certainly began in Africa among our bipedal ancestors, long before the successful exodus of our species into other parts of the world some 80,000 years ago.

Later, hunter-gatherers in groups of 10 to 50 were adept at living off the land, surviving on animals they hunted as well as eating leaves, berries, roots, fruits and nuts. They wandered the land in search of seasonal food, sometimes following migratory herds, while coastal peoples used the resources offered by the sea.

This wandering slowly ceased about 10,000 years ago when wild grasses and some animals were domesticated. And with this greater and more reliable flow of food, people ceased to move on continuously; instead they began living in larger groups and started to multiply faster.

Today, most people (certainly in the developed West) get their food from tenuous supply lines steeped in strict financial dictates rather than from local farms and market gardens. This is an eventual recipe for disaster, as many foragers have realized. By becoming a forager – as well as perhaps starting to grow some of your own vegetables and fruit – you will be countering this trend and getting back to the basics of life.

Plant conservation

The need to conserve and protect native plants for future generations is a responsibility we must all take seriously. Each year, hundreds of species of wild plants around the world are lost to us through habitat loss, greed on the part of some plant collectors and through ignorance. Whatever the cause, this trend needs to be halted. Apart from local fields, roadsides and hedges, many other man-made places provide homes to plants. Towpaths along canals dug centuries ago are full of plants, while disused railways provide not only footpaths and cycle trails but have become ribbons of flourishing plant life. Banking alongside motorways also gives protection to plants, but plants along busy roads cannot be foraged for obvious reasons – the dangers of pollution and fast-moving traffic.

How the plants are arranged

This forager's handbook is organized to enable readers to gain instant information. It is divided into seven parts:

• Edible wild plants, include Chickweed, Dandelions and Stinging Nettles, which are often the bane of gardeners.

• Popular wayside kitchen herbs are often escapees from earlier herb gardens. These include Caraway, Fennel and Spearmint.

• Wild fruits can still be found in the wild, in spite of the fact that many are widely grown as cultivated fruits. These include Blackcurrants, Cranberries and Gooseberries.

• Wild Nuts, borne by trees such as Beech, Hazel and Oak, are edible and collectable. You might also see them growing in hedgerows.

• Mushrooms, truffles and other edible fungi can be gathered and eaten. Most grow at soil-level, some on trees and a few under ground. For safety's sake, careful identification of all fungi is absolutely necessary.

• Seaweeds are gathered along shorelines or just beneath low water and provide highly nutritious meals.

• Shellfish, including Clams, Cockles and Winkles, can be collected from the wild.

The use of common and botanical names

Plants are arranged in alphabetical order according to their most popular common name within each chapter and the botanical name follows its common one. Additionally, because plants (as well as shellfish) are often native to wide areas of the world, they may have gathered many more common names, which are also listed. Therefore, if you only know the common name of a particular plant or shellfish you will be able to find it in the index and then establish where it is described and illustrated. Additionally, where earlier botanical names are still used, these will be included as well – a great help where plants are known and identified through earlier floras and gardening books.

Most native plants have a multitude of common names but, surprisingly, coastal plants such as Sea Purslane have fewer variations than plants that populate inland habitats. It is significant that plants notorious for their invasive habits, such as Ground Elder, have an abundance of common names throughout their habitats.

Foraging code

These simple guidelines will make a big difference to plant life in your area.

✳ Do not strip plants of all their leaves, fruits or nuts. Gather a few leaves or fruits or nuts from each plant. Use a knife or scissors to remove them cleanly. Harvest fungi by carefully twisting the stem and then pulling slightly.

✳ Do not remove flowers from annual or biennial plants as the plant relies on these parts to produce new plants and fruits for the following year.

✳ Do not dig up plants – it's illegal.

✳ When searching for a plant, do not trample over surrounding plants as you may destroy them.

✳ Be aware of the fact that many species of plants are endangered and rare. Gather only those that you know grow in abundance, and do not over-forage. Leave most plants where you find them in order to benefit wild animals and insects.

Correct identification

It is essential to know precisely what you are gathering in order to avoid poisonous plants, and this applies equally to leafy wayside plants as well as to fungi. Therefore, always be certain about the plants you gather and, if in doubt, leave them alone.

Correctly identifying and gathering plants are skills that take time to acquire. Where to look, the time of year the plants are available, and what parts to gather and eat safely are the main questions asked by foragers. But there are also issues of legality that need to be addressed when collecting plants from the wild (see below).

Try to begin foraging with someone who knows what they are doing; learning by observing on the spot with a knowledgeable guide is the best way to acquire safe foraging skills.

Questions of legality

In many countries, wild plants are protected in law and uprooting native plants is illegal, unless permission is first gained from the landowner or occupier. Additionally, permission is especially required to forage for wild plants in nature reserves, in national parks, on land owned by national land organizations and land owned by military establishments.

Wayside plants have long escaped the legality question and foragers are usually free to remove (in moderate amounts) flowers, leaves, fruits (berries and nuts) and fungi from verges and banks alongside town and country roads. Path edges can also be legally foraged.

Remember that foraging just a few plants for your own personal use is usually not a problem, but creating an industry from your gathering is questionable, and you would certainly need permission from the landowner or occupier.

Occasionally you will come across signs that say 'Trespassers will be prosecuted'. The intentions and liabilities of such signs vary from one country to another and it has been suggested that they are meaningless in law unless actual damage is committed. However, to avoid problems arising needlessly, gain permission before foraging on private land. Always ask yourself if the land belonged to you, would you want people walking over it without permission?

Ensuring plants are clean

There are many ways that wild plants can become contaminated, so take care:

• Plants alongside roads are frequently coated by petrol and diesel fumes.
• Wild animals and dogs are inclined to urinate on easily reached plants. Large-leaved plants alongside footpaths are especially at risk from dogs.
• Chemical sprays can contaminate wild plants that grow close to crops. Increasingly, however, farmers are leaving wider areas around cultivated crops to encourage wildlife – especially bees and other insects.

After gathering

Apart from identifying and gathering plants safely, getting them home intact requires care. Leaves need a wide basket that does not constrict them. Berries and nuts, however, need containers that can be closed to prevent them spilling and rolling out.

Cover your basket to prevent the sun and wind from drying your gatherings, and wash and dry leaves (if dirty) as soon as you get them home. Place them in a cool shaded room, away from direct and strong sunlight. Some plants and fruits do not require washing and this is explained in the text for each plant.

Foraging directory

The following pages provide an extensive directory of plants (and some shellfish) that can be foraged. Over 100 species, both wild and escapees from gardens are included, along with tips on identification, where to find them, what and when to harvest and how to prepare and use the plant (or shellfish).

Edible
wild plants

The major wild plants for foraging are represented here. Some are becoming rare in the wild – even though they've been widely and intensively cultivated for centuries – so when foraging treat these rarer species, and all plants for that matter, with respect and restraint.

Among the wild plants fit for foraging are the ancestors of many of our modern-day vegetables. One of these is Wild Cabbage (see page 36); over several centuries and with careful selection by seed companies, it has yielded brassicas as diverse as Brussels Sprouts and Cauliflowers, as well as Cabbages, Kohlrabi and Broccoli. Similarly, Spinach Beet (see page 37) has left a legacy of vegetables, some with large and nutrition-packed swollen roots for feeding cattle, others useful for processing into sugar, as well as succulent and richly colourful roots for adding to salads.

In earlier centuries, because of their value as food crops, many native European plants were introduced to other countries by settlers. Most plants survived and flourished in these new habitats and in some cases were too successful. In New Zealand, for instance, introduced Watercress has become a serious problem when it blocks waterways.

Asparagus (*Asparagus officinalis*)
Also known as: Common Asparagus, Wild Asparagus

A delicious and distinctive perennial with spreading roots that allow it to produce new stems each year. There are two forms and only the upright one, growing up to about 1.5 m (5 ft), is abundant enough to be gathered. Its stiff stems are generously clad in needle-like cladodes – botanically speaking, flattened leaf-like stems – and from a distance have a fern-like appearance. Male flowers (yellow, tinged red at base) and female (yellow to whitish-green) are usually borne on separate plants from early to late summer. Round, red berries about 6 mm (¼ in) wide appear slightly later.

The upright form (*A. o.* ssp. *officinalis*) is native to the warmer parts of Europe, Asia and North Africa, as well as naturalized in parts of North America. It has been introduced into many other countries for cultivation as a food plant, from where it has escaped.

You'll find it: in grassy areas, especially in coastal regions, on cliffs or in dunes and where the soil is light and well drained.

Spears: edible parts of asparagus are the spear-like young shoots that appear in spring and through early or mid-summer. Asparagus in the wild is not so large and prolific as that grown in vegetable gardens that can be cut when about 23 cm (9 in) high.

Harvesting the spears: only harvest in areas where there is a plentiful supply of spears (it is scarce in some areas). Where there are sufficient spears to harvest, use a long-bladed knife to cut the base just below soil-level.

Using the spears: wash and re-cut the bases, then either steam or poach in water until just tender. Asparagus spears are versatile in the kitchen and can be used in many dishes, including fondues, risottos, quiches, soups and salads. Asparagus is also delicious steamed and served simply, either drizzled with melted butter, vinaigrette or a hollandaise sauce.

Chickweed (*Stellaria media*)

Also known as: Chicken's Meat, Chickenweed, Stitchwort

Birds and chickens love to peck at the flowers and seeds of this widespread and abundant sprawling annual, which persists throughout winter in mild climates. It spreads and forms masses of leaves on weak stems that creep over the soil, forming clumps up to 35 cm (14 in) but usually less.

The plant produces white, star-like flowers about 9 mm (³⁄₈ in) across throughout the year, but mainly in summer. With a cosmopolitan nature, it is found throughout the world; indeed, claims have been made that it is the most widespread and abundant of all wild plants.

You'll find it: on bare ground, especially in light, cultivated soil where seeds quickly germinate and create carpets of leaves, stems and flowers.

Leaves: the abundant soft, bright green oval leaves clasp stems; as they age, they become darker and tougher.

Harvesting the leaves: if tugged sharply, whole stems complete with soil-covered roots are pulled up, so use sharp scissors to cut off only the young, leaf-clad stems. If they appear dirty, wash and allow to dry.

Using the leaves: young leaves have a mild flavour and can be eaten raw in salads, when they are at their best. Young stems are just as tender as the leaves and can also be eaten, although some people remove them. Add the leaves to scrambled eggs, use in soups or gently soften in butter which makes their flavour resemble spring spinach.

In times of scarcity, Chickweed seeds have been ground to a fine powder and used to make bread or to thicken soups; the leaves were picked, dried and infused in boiling water to make a tea.

Chicory (*Cichorium intybus*)

Also known as: Barbe-de-Capuchin, Blue Daisy, Blue Endive, Blue-sailors, Bunk, Coffee Weed, Common Chicory, Succory, Wild Succory, Witloof

A well-known perennial with a long taproot and stiffly erect, grooved stems to 90 cm (3 ft), chicory is native to many regions – much of Europe, western Asia and North Africa. It has been introduced to eastern Asia, North and South America, South Africa, Australia and New Zealand. The roots are eaten as a vegetable, the leaves used in salads and flowers as a garnish. The roots are also used as a coffee substitute.

You'll find it: in grassy areas and on wasteland, especially on chalk, alongside old vegetable gardens and allotments and near derelict country cottages.

Roots, leaves and flower heads: the light-brown roots are 45 cm (18 in) or more long when in light, deeply cultivated soil and somewhat shorter when growing in heavy soil. Basal leaves above the root's top are spear-shaped and stalkless while upper ones clasp upright, stiff stems. Stems bear azure-blue daisy-like flowers from early summer to early autumn.

Chicory coffee To use as a coffee substitute, clean, peel and chop up the roots into 7.5 cm (3 in) long pieces, then roast under a grill until deep brown, firm and crisp. When completely cool, grind the crisp roots in a coffee grinder or food processor to form coffee-like granules or powder. Chicory is highly prized in some countries as it produces a coffee with a deep colour and does not contain caffeine. Occasionally, it is blended with 'true' coffee.

Harvesting roots and leaves: roots are best dug up in late autumn, when the leaves are dying down. However, unless you have permission from the landowner, it is illegal to dig up plants growing in the wild. Pick young, fresh leaves for salads, washing and drying before using. Flowers, for garnish, should be picked when young and fresh.

Using the roots and leaves: apart from a coffee substitute, roots can be grated and added to salads, or eaten as a cooked vegetable; reduce their bitterness by boiling for the second time in fresh water. Some people, however, prefer the bitter taste.

Using the leaves: add to summer salads.

Comfrey (*Symphytum officinale*)

Also known as: Back-wort, Boneset, Bruisewort, Church Bells, Common Comfrey, Healing Herb, Knitbone, Pigweed

Growing 1.2 m (4 ft) high, Comfrey is a bushy herbaceous perennial famed for its ability to grow in low temperatures and its prodigious yield of leaves, which are used to feed cattle. Its cream-white, mauve, yellowish-white or pink bell-shaped flowers are borne in clusters during late spring and early summer. Native to much of Europe and Asia, it has been taken to other countries, including North America, as animal fodder and has escaped into the wild and become naturalized.

In addition to its fodder qualities, comfrey is widely recommended in country cures, including reducing pain, healing broken bones, as a poultice and to relieve coughs.

Comfrey soup

- Make a white sauce as a base, using 25 g (1 oz) margarine or butter, 25 g (1 oz) plain flour and 600 ml (20 fl oz) milk.
- Then add 3–4 tbsp of finely chopped comfrey leaves, which have first been lightly cooked in butter as you would spinach.
- Add a crumbled stock cube (chicken or vegetable) and 300 ml (10 fl oz) water to the soup, then correct the seasonings to taste. Bring the soup to a gentle boil and stir for a few minutes before serving with crusty bread or croutons.

You'll find it: especially in damp areas alongside wet ditches, streams and rivers; also at the edges of fields where it was once cultivated.

Leaves: masses of broad, spear-shaped, hairy-surfaced, mid-green leaves up to 25 cm (10 in) long.

Harvesting the leaves: cut young leaves from plants and wash before use.

Using the leaves: when dipped in batter and fried, Comfrey is claimed to be one of the tastiest delights for foragers. The stems and leaves can be boiled in the same way as cabbage. The older leaves have as much flavour as younger ones in cooked dishes, but the young leaves are picked in spring to add to salads.

Curled Dock (*Rumex crispus*)

Also known as: Curly Dock, Narrow-leaf
Dock, Sour Dock, Yellow Dock

An upright herbaceous perennial that grows
to about 1 m (3½ ft) with stems of densely
clustered tiny flowers from early summer to
mid-autumn that turn a rich brown after they start
to produce seeds. The shiny brown seeds have a
covering that allows them to float on water as well
as to be caught in wool and animal fur, enabling plants to
spread easily and rapidly. Indeed, in some areas this plant is
treated as a pest as it invades cultivated crops.

It is widely seen in Europe and Africa, as well as spreading to other
regions, including North America, where it is naturalized in some areas.

Edible docks Several related
species are ideal for foraging,
including Sorrel (see page 33).
Other docks include *Rumex
obtusifolius*, the Broad-leaved
Dock, with leaves that can
be eaten when young but are
usually more bitter than Curled
Dock. It is also known as Butter
Dock because its long, broad
leaves were used to wrap
around butter to keep it cool
and fresh.

Monk's rhubarb (*Rumex alpinus*,
earlier known as *Rumex pseudo-
alpinus*) is native to central and
southern Europe and parts
of Asia; in the Middle Ages it
was used as a pot herb, when
young leaves were eaten fresh.
It is now naturalized in many
countries, including North
America.

You'll find it: in a wide range of habitats,
including shingle beaches, sand dunes, on
wasteland, cultivated soil, and in grassy areas.
Leaves: dark green, lance-shaped and wavy
edged. Unlike some docks, the lower leaves are
not distinctively heart-shaped at their bases.
Harvesting the leaves: preferably cut when
the leaves are young, at the base, and use
immediately before they flag and become limp.
Using the leaves: add fresh young leaves to
salads – wash and dry first to ensure they are not
contaminated by animals. Old leaves are usually
too bitter to be eaten fresh, but can be boiled in
several changes of water to make them palatable;
use these as a green vegetable.
Young leaves are often cooked like spinach to
accompany ham or bacon; either blanch the leaves
quickly in a little water or sauté with a small knob
of butter, then add a tiny amount of vinegar and
season with salt and pepper.

Dandelion (*Taraxacum officinale*)
Also known as: Clock Flower, Clocks and Watches, Common Dandelion

This well-known perennial can be foraged for its leaves and for the roots that make a passable substitute coffee. Flowers are golden-yellow, often 5 cm (2 in) or more across and borne singly at the tops of hollow, soft stems. A truly cosmopolitan plant, Dandelion is abundant throughout the Northern Hemisphere. Additionally, it has been taken to many other regions as a food plant, where it has become naturalized.

You'll find it: in meadows, pastures, lawns, wasteground, gardens and alongside roads.

Leaves and roots: light green leaves, 25 cm (10 in) long that develop from the plant's base and reveal deeply indented edges.

Harvesting leaves and roots: snap off or cut young leaves from near the base; towards the end of summer they toughen and are less appetizing. Harvest roots in autumn when fat and starting to harden. They are so common that you may well be able to dig them from your own garden. Avoid those along country paths and roadsides, since they may be contaminated by dogs and exhaust fumes respectively.

Using leaves and roots: add young leaves to salads; wash thoroughly then trim off stem bases. By picking from young plants, it is possible to have salad leaves all summer. Crispy bacon pieces added to a dandelion salad makes a delicious combination.

To make coffee, gather roots, wash and trim tops and bottoms. Do not peel, just brush under a tap until clean. Place in full sun to dry, then roast in a moderate oven until brittle. Grind coarsely. Many believe it is almost undistinguishable from real coffee, with the bonus of not containing caffeine.

A feast of possibilities
Dandelions offer foragers even more prizes: in early summer young roots can be boiled and added to salads, while young flower buds can be eaten fresh in salads or boiled. Mature flowers can be cooked in batter or used to brew dandelion wine (there are numerous recipes to be found in old cookery books and on the web).

Fat Hen (*Chenopodium album*)

Also known as: Bacon Weed, Frost-blite, Goosefoot, Lamb's Quarters, Meal-weed, Pigweed, Wild Spinach, White Goosefoot

This common annual grows up to 60 cm (2 ft) high, from widely scattered seeds produced by flowers that appear from early summer to mid-autumn. This unprepossessing plant has filled stomachs since early man roamed the landscape. It is widespread in Europe and Asia, North and South Africa, Australia and North America. It spreads readily and creates colonies.

You'll find it: on wasteland as well as in cultivated soil, along the edges of fields, on rubbish heaps and the sides of ditches. It is abundant on disturbed soil especially that which is friable and moisture-retentive, where the seeds germinate easily and young plants grow.

Leaves and seeds: pale greyish-green leaves are usually lance-shaped but can be variable and with a diamond outline. Young leaves have a mealy-white covering, and rise directly from main stems that are usually green but sometimes reddish. The leaves are rich in iron, vitamins and calcium. The small black round or kidney-shaped seeds are tightly clustered in spikes towards the top of stems. Individual plants can produce as many as 75,000 seeds.

Harvesting and using leaves and seeds: gather young leaves and shoots in spring and early summer for cooking like spinach; use as a green vegetable or add to soups. Alternatively, use fresh in salads. Later in summer, young leaves can be used in a similar way; with age, those lower down become bitter and unpalatable. When gathering seeds, cut off entire stems with their seeds attached and put the heads upside down in a paper bags. Seeds will eventually fall off and can be gathered and used, either as a cereal or ground into a black flour and made into bread, which is highly nutritious.

Good King Henry (*Chenopodium bonus-henricus*)

Also known as: **All Good, Goosefoot, Lancashire Asparagus, Mercury, Perennial Goosefoot, Wild Spinach**

This erect herbaceous perennial grows to 50 cm (20 in) high, with a bushy and slightly spreading nature, and is popular as a green vegetable. From late spring to mid-summer plants develop tapering and pyramidal heads of small green flowers. It is native to Europe and Asia, and has also been introduced as a food plant to many countries, including North America. The plant has become naturalized and widespread in many countries.

You'll find it: around old gardens, fields and allotments, along the sides of country roads and especially in areas close to old cottages where it might earlier have been cultivated. It likes fertile, moisture-retentive soil.
Leaves: normally up to 10 cm (4 in) long and clustered around upright stems, the leaves are somewhat fleshy, triangular-shaped and a lustrous green.
Harvesting the leaves: cut the leaves while young, throughout the summer, severing them at the base. Although it has a succulent nature, leaves soon go limp once picked, therefore do not pick more leaves than you can use that same day.
Using the leaves: trim off long stems from the bases of leaves and wash thoroughly under running water, then boil or steam in the same way you might cook spinach. Because of its high oxalic acid content, eat in moderation (although it is also rich in iron and vitamin C). Early in the year (usually during late spring and early summer), gather young shoots and steam or cook these in a similar way to asparagus.

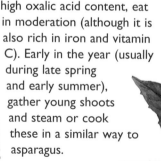

Cooking flower buds and young shoots

- Wash the buds and young shoots thoroughly and simmer in a saucepan for five minutes in just enough boiling water to cover. Alternatively you could steam them to retain nutrients.
- Drain well and pour over some melted butter and serve on toast.

Goosegrass (*Galium aparine*)

Also known as: Bedstraw, Catchweed, Catch-weed Bedstraw, Cleavers, Clivers, Common Cleavers, Hairif, Hayriff, Sticky Willie

A sprawling annual with prostrate or scrambling branched stems up to 1 m (3½ ft) long, with groups of leaves at intervals along the stems. Small stems arise from the leaf-joints and bear tiny, dull-white flowers from early to late summer. The stems have numerous small, down-turned prickles that cling to clothing and fur, giving rise to many of the plant's common names.

It is widespread in Europe and north and western Asia, as well as having been taken and naturalized in many countries.

You'll find it: in hedges and on wasteland, in ditches, shady thickets, on cultivated land and in coastal areas.

Leaves: at intervals along the stems, six to eight, light to mid-green, narrow and pointed leaves arise in clusters.

Harvesting the leaves: these are best when young and easily cut from the plant, together with their stems, with a sharp knife or scissors. If just pulled, the entire plant becomes dislodged. Cut and use the leaves and stems before the hard, round seeds appear.

Using the leaves: boil both the leaves and stems in water for a few seconds to remove the plant's clinging nature and make the leaves and stems palatable. It can be used as a green vegetable and is very high in vitamin C – in earlier times it was used to keep scurvy at bay. In the 17th century the leaves and stems were recommended for use in puddings and spring soups.

Coffee substitute The seeds of goosegrass can be roasted to produce a coffee substitute. Collect and dry the seeds well, then roast until brown in a medium oven. They can then be ground and used to make a hot drink.

Ground Elder (*Aegopodium podagraria*)

Also known as: Ash-weed, Bishop's Gout-weed, Bishop's Weed, Farmer's Plague, Goat's Foot, Goutweed, Ground Ash, Herb Gerard, Parson's Weed, Snow-in-the-Mountain

To many people this is one of the most pernicious garden weeds. It has an herbaceous perennial nature, with creeping roots that enable it to spread and colonize land, therefore eating it can be considered an act of common justice! Growing to 1 m (3½ ft) or less, it has hollow stems that bear the leaves, and from early to late summer, white flowers in umbrella-like heads.

Native to Europe, southern Turkey, the Caucasus and Siberia, it was introduced to other countries as a food and medicinal plant (invariably against gout). It is established in North America and many other countries, where initially it was cultivated as a pot herb.

You'll find it: on waste areas, especially near old buildings and gardens. Also look at the base of hedges and alongside roads.

Leaves: are 10–20 cm (4–8 in) long, medium to dark green and usually formed of three finely tooth-edged leaflets.

Harvesting the leaves: young leaves are the best and tastiest, picked in spring and early summer. However, pinching out flower shoots helps to protract the season when young leaves appear. Collect leaves before the plants flower, as after that time they have a strongly laxative nature.

Using the leaves: wash the leaves thoroughly under running water, then allow to dry in the air. Ground elder leaves can be used in a wide range of dishes and preparations, including soups, quiches, fritters and omelettes. These can also be steamed and used much like spinach. Add young leaves to salads, where they impart an aromatic and rather tangy flavour.

Jack-by-the-Hedge (*Alliaria petiolata*)

Also known as: Garlic Mustard, Garlic Root, Hedge Garlic, Jack in the Bush, Jack-in-the-Hedge, Penny Hedge, Poor Man's Mustard, Sauce Alone

An erect annual or biennial with a slender taproot that smells strongly of garlic when crushed. In mild and warm areas it flowers in early spring, producing early seeds that fall and germinate later in the same year; these create a further display of plants, but this is not the norm. Clusters of white flowers appear at the tops of stems from mid-spring to early summer.

Native throughout Europe, southern Turkey, North Africa and as far as the Caucusus and Himalayas, it has been introduced to many other areas, including North America from Canada to Virginia.

You'll find it: at the sides of hedges and walls, along the edges of woods and in shaded gardens.
Leaves: long-stalked, bright green leaves with heart-shaped bases that emit a garlic-like aroma when bruised.
Harvesting the leaves: cut off young leaves when wanted and use as soon as possible as these tend to wilt quickly. Each plant has only a few leaves so select only a very few at a time from each plant.
Using the leaves: clusters of flowers, but primarily the leaves can be eaten fresh in spring and early summer salads. Additionally, the leaves can be used in a sauce to accompany lamb and herrings. Create the sauce by chopping fresh young leaves together with a little mint, and mix with sugar and vinegar. The leaves can also be chopped and added to soups and meat casseroles.

Lovage (*Levisticum officinale*)

Also known as: Cornish Lovage, Italian Lovage, King's Cumin, Old English Lovage

A tall herbaceous perennial about 1.2–1.5 m (4–5 ft) high with large, dark green leaves, it displays greenish-yellow flowers in large, umbrella-like heads from early to late summer.

Native to Mediterranean regions, the Balkans, India and southern Asia, it has been taken to many warm and temperate countries as a culinary herb, from where it has escaped and become naturalized. It is widely seen in North America.

You'll find it: in damp soil, often around neglected herb gardens and allotments.

Leaves, stems and seeds: the segmented leaves are large and formed of glossy, broad, coarsely toothed lobes, especially towards their tops. The stems are stiff and upright, while the yellow-brown seeds are egg-shaped.

Harvesting the leaves, stems and seeds: snip off the leaves while still young, together with young stems. Stems, which are hollow, can be candied and are therefore cut off slightly later. To gather seeds, wait until the flowers fade and the seeds are yellow-brown. Then, cut off the stems so that the seed heads can be placed upside down in a paper bag and the stems hung up. When dry, seeds will fall into the bag.

Using the leaves, stems and seeds: when young, use the leaves in salads, stir-fries, soups and potato dishes. They can also be added to stews. Lovage butter, a fusion of butter, finely chopped leaves plus pepper and salt is ideal as a dressing for corn on the cob.

Leaf stalks when young are eaten fresh or candied. The seeds are used, whole or crushed, in cakes, biscuits or sweets. Additionally, they are added to meat and cheese dishes and salad dressings to add flavour. Grated roots are ideal for adding to salads or cooked as a vegetable. It has a similar flavour to celery.

Meadowsweet (*Filipendula ulmaria*)

Also known as: Maids of the Meadow, Meadow-sweet, Meadows Queen, Meadwort, Queen of the Meadow

An herbaceous perennial up to 1.2 m (4 ft) high with long-stemmed leaves, it has large, dense, umbrella-like heads of creamy-white flowers that emit a sweet but sickly fragrance from early summer to early autumn.

Native throughout Europe, from Iceland to Arctic Russia, Asia and southern Turkey to Mongolia, it is seen as an escapee and naturalized in eastern parts of North America.

You'll find it: in wet, damp woods and meadows; also in marshes and fens and alongside streams and ditches.

Leaves: pleasantly aromatic, dark green leaves, each formed of two to five pairs of tooth-edged leaflets. Leaves have greyish-white undersides.

Harvesting the leaves: cut while young and fresh and before eaten by insects.

Using the leaves and flowers: chop up young leaves and use to flavour soups. Dried leaves have been used to introduce aromatic aromas to wines, as well as to mead. Flowers when added to beer and wine are claimed to make a stronger and more heady brew, and introduces sweetness when used in cold drinks and fruit salads during summer.

Medicinal values Young leaves and flowers are occasionally infused together to make a tea that is claimed to ease the common cold, soothe inflammatory problems and calm stomach complaints. The plant contains the chemicals that are used to produce aspirin.

Perennial Stinging Nettle (*Urtica dioica*)

Also known as: Devil's Leaf, Devil's Plaything, European Nettle, Slender Nettle, Stinging Nettle, Tall Nettle

A well-known herbaceous perennial, 1.2 m (4 ft) or more high, with tough yellow branching and spreading roots, it develops green flowers with yellow stamens in catkin-like arrangements from early to late summer. It appears throughout temperate regions of the world.

You'll find it: in hedgerows, on grassy banks and wasteland, in woods and especially close to rubbish heaps and old abandoned buildings, where it forms near-impenetrable colonies.

Leaves: upright stems, seldom branching, are covered with stinging hairs and bear green, somewhat heart-shaped, tooth-edged leaves that also impart a sting when touched.

Harvesting the leaves: wear gloves and cut off the top 15 cm (6 in) of young stems only to the end of early summer; after that the leaves become tough, have a bitter taste and laxative properties.

Using the leaves: always wash the leaves under running water before preparing them for boiling or, preferably, steaming for about four minutes. These leaves, which are high in vitamins A and C, iron and protein, can be used as a green vegetable as well as made into a purée – this is particularly good served on toast with the addition of a poached egg. Nettle soup is a delicious summertime forager's treat and nettles can be included in any recipe for which you would use spinach.

Nettle soup

Collect enough nettle tops and leaves to half-fill a carrier bag, then wash carefully. Soften 2 chopped onions, 2 chopped celery sticks and a crushed garlic clove in a small knob of butter in a large saucepan. Then add 1 litre (34 fl oz) vegetable or chicken stock and all the nettles you can cram into your pan. Bring to the boil and simmer for ten minutes or so until the nettles are tender. Purée the soup in a blender or food processor, return to the pan briefly and add 3–4 tablepoons crème fraiche or cream. Heat through, correct the seasonings and serve.

Rock Samphire (*Crithmum maritimum*)

Also known as: Samphire, Crest Marine, Rock Semper, Sea Bean, Sea Samphire

Succulent branching perennial with a slightly woody base, the plant can be recognized by its warm, slightly sulphurous scent. It grows 15–38 cm (6–15 in) high, with a sprawling nature, especially if in a position open to the wind. The leaves are grey-green, with tiny, yellowish-green flowers borne in umbrella-like arrangements from early to late summer.

Native to the Atlantic coast of Europe, Mediterranean regions, Black Sea, Madeira, Azores and Canaries, it has been taken to many other countries, including North America and Australia, where it is often found as an escapee. It is still grown in herb gardens.

You'll find it: usually on sea cliffs and in rocky, well-drained coastal areas and occasionally in gravely and sandy soil.

Leaves: firm and formed of several cylindrical, fleshy, narrow, tapering segments, each up to 5 cm (2 in) long.

Harvesting the leaves: cut the leaf stems carefully, taking care not to pull them and to tear the plant from its roots. This is best done in spring or early summer, before the flowers appear.

Using the leaves: both the aromatic young leaves and their stems can be eaten. First, however, remove and discard those that have turned slimy, together with any hard parts on the stems. Wash the leaves thoroughly under running water and boil in water for about ten minutes or until soft, then eat as you would asparagus, with butter.

In earlier years, young leaves were especially prized and often pickled; they were first salted, then boiled and when soft covered with spiced vinegar. Another recipe suggests pickling them with shallots, cloves, mace and black mustard seeds to add further flavour. In some coastal areas, leaves were cooked and eaten with bread.

Salad Burnet (*Sanguisorba minor*)

Also known as: **Burnet, Drum Sticks, Garden Burnet, Old Man's Pepper, Poor Man's Pepper**

This upright herbaceous perennial grows 15–60 cm (6–24 in) high and from late spring to late summer develops rounded flower heads about 12 mm (½ in) wide, packed with greenish-white flowers, often with purplish tinges. However, it is the leaves that are the main culinary attraction.

It is native to large parts of Europe, North Africa, the Canary Islands and southwest and central Asia; it was introduced into North America by early European settlers and has become widely naturalized.

You'll find it: in dry, grassy places, especially where the soil is chalky.
Leaves: formed of four to twelve pairs of greyish-green leaflets with coarsely saw-toothed edges. When crushed they emit the refreshing aroma of cucumbers.
Harvesting the leaves: young leaves have the best flavour, becoming bitter as they age. Use as fresh as possible, before the leaves start to wilt.
Using the leaves: if dirty, wash in clean water and allow to dry. Use whole in salads and added to cool summer drinks, especially in punches, where their cucumber-like flavour has a cooling influence.

The leaves of this distinctive plant have many other uses, including chopped and added to soups, in sauces for fish dishes and in casseroles. Additionally, leaves are used in vinegars and salad dressings, as well as finely cut up and sprinkled over steamed vegetables. It combines well with Rosemary (see page 51) and Tarragon.

Scotch Lovage (*Ligusticum scoticum*)

Also known as: Lovage, Scots Lovage, Sea Lovage, Sea Parsley

This herbaceous perennial, growing up to 90 cm (3 ft) high, has ribbed stems, usually green but occasionally tinted magenta-purple at the base, and has a celery-like aroma when crushed. Umbrella-like heads, up to 6 cm (2½ in) across, bear greenish-white to yellow flowers during early and mid-summer. The egg-shaped seeds are ridged. It is native to northern Europe and as far north as the Arctic Circle and to Greenland and North America.

You'll find it: on rocky cliffs and on shingle close to the seashore.

Leaves: up to 10 cm (4 in) long and formed of five to ten oval segments, sometimes lobed. Like the stems, the coarsely tooth-edged, bright green, shiny leaves have a strong celery-like scent.

Harvesting the leaves: snip off only a few at a time, as in some areas this plant is scarce.

Using the leaves and stems: in earlier years, this robust plant was grown as a pot herb, and during times of scarcity the leaves have sustained people and helped to avert scurvy. Shred young leaves and add to early summer salads, and use to add body to soups. The leaves can also be wrapped around joints of meat for roasting. In a similar way to Angelica, the hollow stems can be candied, as well as blanched and stewed. In earlier years, the seeds were added to soups, stews and meat to add a sharp, hot flavour. Indeed, using seeds as a flavouring was popular when pepper was expensive.

Sea Kale (*Crambe maritima*)

Also known as: Scurvy Grass, Sea Cabbage, Sea Colewort, Seakale

This cabbage-like perennial has erect stems about 90 cm (3 ft) high, and fleshy roots that send up young shoots that are much sought-after by foragers. However, only take a few shoots as these plants are relatively scarce in the wild.

The large lower leaves, up to 30 cm (12 in) long, are fleshy and rounded with crinkly lobes and irregularly toothed edges. The upper leaves are smaller, usually narrow and without indentations. Lax and open clusters of white flowers with green claws appear from early to late summer.

It is native to the Atlantic coast of Europe, from northern Spain to Oslo, along the Baltic coast and round the Black Sea.

You'll find it: on cliffs, along coastal sands and at the tops of shingle beaches.

Leaf stalks: these are the desired parts and often become naturally blanched when sand and shingle are swept around the bases. In earlier years, local people waited for the first signs of it in late winter and early spring and then drew sand and shingle around the bases to cause blanching. This both whitened the stalks and decreased their bitterness. It can be cut and eaten in late spring and early summer.

Harvesting leaf stalks: cut young clustered leaf stalks when about 13–15 cm (5–6 in) high, using a sharp knife to sever the stalk fractionally below the ground's surface. Preferably, these young shoots are cut when the leaves are barely developed.

Using leaf stalks: these have a nutty and slightly bitter flavour and are usually cut into 7.5 cm (3 in) lengths and boiled in salted water until tender (15–20 minutes) or steamed like asparagus for five or so minutes until *al dente*. Serve with a butter sauce or lemon juice. Very young shoots can be shredded and eaten fresh in salads.

Sea Purslane (*Atriplex portulacoides*)

You might find this well-branched, small evergreen shrub with creeping roots listed as *Halimione portulacoides* or even *Obione portulacoides* in old floras and gardening books. It has a spreading nature with branches creeping and developing roots at their stem joints.

From mid-summer to early autumn it develops terminal clusters of flowers in short, branching spires. When in bud, they are reddish, but soon turning green. However, it is the golden-yellow pollen that gives the plant a bright appearance. It is native throughout Europe from Denmark southwards, and also found in North Africa, southern Turkey and South Africa. It has been introduced into North America, where it has colonized large areas near the Atlantic coast.

You'll find it: in salt marshes, alongside coastal water channels and at the edges of salty pools. It also survives when flooded with seawater at high tide.

Leaves: oval, mealy-covered, fleshy and grey-green, with silvery undersides. These are borne on upright, brownish stems to about 75 cm (2½ ft), but usually slightly less.

Harvesting the leaves: cut young, fleshy leaves individually, taking care not to damage the plant by taking too many leaves.

Using the leaves: trim off hard basal parts and wash thoroughly in running water to remove any excess salt and tideline debris. They are small and have a crunchy texture. Either eat raw in salads or stir-fry to accompany meat and fish dishes, however, take care not to cook excessively as this destroys the texture.

Earlier it was grown as a pot herb so that the young leaves could be readily picked.

Sorrel (*Rumex acetosa*)

Also known as: **Bread and Cheese,
Common Sorrel, Garden Sorrel,
Green Sorrel, Sour Dock, Spinach Dock**

This erect herbaceous perennial grows to about
1 m (3½ ft) with a clump-forming nature and has
masses of arrow-shaped leaves. From late spring
to late summer it develops slightly branched stems
bearing spires of small red and green flowers. For
centuries it has been eaten as a green vegetable, largely
because of its lemon-like flavour.

It is native and widespread to Europe, temperate Asia,
Greenland and North America. It has been taken to many
countries as a food plant, where it has escaped and naturalized.

Sorrel sauce Creating recipes
for sorrel sauces appears to
have been a cottage industry in
earlier years. Many were created
to serve with fish, utilizing the
cooling, lemony flavour of the
leaves to produce a green sauce.
Leaves were chopped and boiled
with very little water, then
mixed with sugar and vinegar.
A sauce made solely from the
leaves was used to accompany
pork or goose when apples
were scarce.

You'll find it: in grassland,
meadows and open woodland; also
along roadsides and in ditches.

Leaves: up to 10 cm (4 in) long with an
arrow-like outline; each leaf has distinctive
downward-pointing lobes as its base. High
in vitamin C and oxalic acid (which can be
toxic in high doses).

Harvesting the leaves: cut the stems
of young leaves at the base; this gives later
emerging leaves a better chance to develop.
Use the leaves as soon as possible, before
they wilt.

Using the leaves: apart from being used
as a green vegetable, it can be cut and added
fresh to salads, where it introduces a lemony
flavour. Additionally, it is delicous in soups and sauces. Its versatility
does not end there, as earlier it was a substitute for apple in tarts and
turnovers. Puréed sorrel has been a popular accompaniment to veal and
fish, as well as being added to omelettes and stews.

Watercress (*Rorippa nasturtium-aquaticum*)
Also known as: Bilders, Butter Cress, Tang-tongues, Tongue Grass

This popular and widespread perennial (occasionally annual), which is also called *Rorippa officinale* and *Nasturtium officinale*, has leaves and stems that are eaten fresh or occasionally boiled. Growing in water, the smooth, angular stems are anchored and secured by roots, while the hollow stems enable the upper parts to float. From late spring to mid-autumn plants produce white-petalled flowers in upward clusters.

Native to southern and central Europe, including much of southern Scandinavia and the Carpathians, North Africa and western Asia, it was introduced into many other countries including North and South America and New Zealand.

You'll find it: in shallow streams and ditches with moving water or on their banks.

Leaves: silky-green and broadly elliptical or round, with uncut edges; the lower leaves have one to three leaflets, while upper ones reveal five to nine, sometimes more. There are several closely related species, but this one has leaves that remain green in autumn, although it is susceptible to damage from winter frost.

Harvesting the leaves: snip off young stems and leaves (do not pull as you may disturb the roots). Be aware that in some areas wild watercress may harbour liver flukes, a harmful parasite.

Using the leaves: wash under a running tap, and do not pick leaves from plants in dirty ditches or those into which farm waste may have drained. Use the leaves while fresh, either as a nibble, in salads and sandwiches or as a garnish. Leaves are especially high in vitamin C and iron. In earlier years it was lightly boiled and used as a green vegetable. It has also been added to stews and soups (where it imparts a pungent flavour), chopped and added to scrambled eggs, or stir-fried with other vegetables.

White Mustard (*Sinapis alba*)
Also known as: Mustard

Known earlier as *Brassica alba* and *Brassica hirta*, this annual is often raised to produce young seedlings to accompany Garden Cress in the popular duo 'mustard and cress'; they are used in sandwiches and salads and as a garnish. But the forager often finds that the plant is more developed, with larger distinctive leaves rather than seedlings.

In the wild, stems grow to about 75 cm (2½ ft) long, sometimes branched and sprawling. From early to late summer, plants develop lax and spire-like heads of lemon-yellow flowers.

Probably native to Mediterranean and western Asia, it is now widespread in Europe, Japan, North and South America as well as New Zealand.

You'll find it: in moisture-retentive cultivated soil and wasteland; often an escapee from cultivation when grown as a food crop for animals or grown as a green manure crop that is later ploughed in to improve soil structure and nutritional qualities. Therefore, look for it at the edges of farmland and in ditches.

Leaves, flower buds and seeds: dull green leaves, stiff and hairy, deeply lobed and up to 15 cm (6 in) long. As they age the leaves become slightly bitter. The flower buds are borne on spikes and the seeds are produced in pods containing yellowish brown seeds.

Harvesting the leaves, flower buds and seeds: pick a few clean leaves for casual eating or a few more for taking home. Wash thoroughly and dry before use. Flower buds should be collected before the flowers open and seeds are collected once the pods have developed and ripened.

Using the leaves, flower buds and seeds: lightly steam or stir-fry both leaves and flower buds, although leaves are best when fresh in salads. The seeds can be used to make mustard or to sprout for use in salads.

Wild Cabbage (*Brassica oleracea*)
Also known as: Sea Cabbage, Sea Cole

This biennial or perennial is the ancestor of our cultivated European brassicas, ranging from Broccoli, Brussels Sprouts and Cauliflowers to Kohlrabi. Although these food plants are certainly distinctive and markedly different from each other, when seen in flower the similarities to their ancestor are readily apparent.

Wild Cabbage usually grows no more than 1 m (3½ ft) high, with lax but clustered spires of yellow flowers from late spring to late summer. It is native to coastal areas of Europe, especially along the Atlantic, as well as Mediterranean and Adriatic shores. Sometimes plants similar to Wild Cabbage can be seen, but these are usually escapees from cultivated forms that have reverted to earlier characteristics.

You'll find it: as some of its common names suggest, it is a maritime plant and widely seen on cliffs, clinging to the sides and tops. It is also found around rocks and on dry-stone walls in coastal areas where it clings

tenuously to life.

Leaves: those at the base of the plant tend to have stalks, are broad, rounded and with lobes. They are slightly thick and fleshy, a characteristic that distinguishes them from related plants such as White Mustard (see page 35) and other related species. The upper leaves partly clasp the stem and do not have lobes. Both types of leaves are greyish-green.

Harvesting the leaves: cut leaves off close to the base of the stalk. Note that this plant is now scarce, so take only a very few leaves at one time.

Using the leaves: at one time, Sea Cabbage was so abundant that it was collected and sold from market stalls. Leaves can be steamed for use as a green vegetable but they are more usually eaten fresh in spite of their bitter taste.

Wild Spinach (*Beta vulgaris* ssp. *maritima*)
Also known as: Sea Beet

Known earlier as *Beta maritima*, this perennial is the ancestor of the many beets that are now grown for animal food, for sugar production and for culinary purposes. Unlike culinary beetroots, Wild Spinach does not have conspicuously swollen areas at the junction of the roots and stems. And instead of being foraged for its roots, its large, fleshy leaves are much sought-after.

Plants grow 75–90 cm (2½–3 ft) high and have narrow spires of tiny green flowers from mid-summer to early autumn. It is native to seashores of Europe, North Africa, the Azores and from southern Turkey to the southeast Asia.

You'll find it: either on the shore or close to shorelines.

Leaves: thick and leathery oval or wedge-shaped and pointed shiny green, often 10 cm (4 in) or more long.

Harvesting the leaves: from late spring to early autumn, use a sharp knife to cut leaves cleanly, close to the base of each leaf-stalk. It is wise to select leaves that are on plants inaccessible to dogs.

Using the leaves: wash leaves thoroughly. If old and have a pronounced central rib down the centre, cut this away. Eat the leaves fresh, shredded and added to salads, as well as cooked as a green vegetable in a similar way to spinach. Young leaves from near the plant's top are best for adding to salads. When cooking large leaves, steam rather than boil. Serve with a knob of butter.

Wild Spinach and lemon salad

This is a popular recipe that reveals the tangy flavour of Wild Spinach.
- Thoroughly wash the leaves and cut away tough stems and central parts.
- Poach the leaves in boiling water for two to three minutes, then rinse in cold water.
- After washing a lemon, slice it paper-thin and position slices around the edge of a plate. Add the Wild Spinach, as well as a few sprigs of Watercress.
- Drizzle with olive oil and coarsely ground black pepper to finish the dish.

Popular wayside kitchen herbs

Wayside kitchen herbs are a cosmopolitan group of plants, native to large parts of the world, particularly the temperate zones that offer a warm and mild environment. Many of these herbs have been grown for thousands of years to add a wide spectrum of flavours to food and to provide herbal remedies.

These culinary delights differ widely in their habits of growth and include annuals, biennials and herbaceous perennials, as well as those with a shrub-like nature. Annual plants reproduce themselves from seeds produced every year, while biennials take two seasons to produce seeds. Herbaceous perennials last from one year to another – the leaves and shoots die down to soil-level in autumn or early winter and in spring produce fresh growth. They owe their perennial nature to their hardy roots and stem bases.

Shrubs have a woody nature and can be evergreen or deciduous. Each shrub has several stems that arise from its roots to form a permanent framework. Rosemary is an excellent example of an evergreen, culinary shrub.

Because many of the culinary herbs featured here have been cultivated for centuries, it is not surprising that they have escaped and colonized areas around houses. Additionally, you might come across them in gardens and areas where old houses have been demolished and all that remains are skeleton walls and fences.

Therefore, herbs can act as a record of an earlier cultivated past in what appears to be barren territory.

Borage (*Borago officinalis*)

Also known as: Burrage, Cool-tankard, Talewort

This stout hollow-stemmed annual, growing to 45–90 cm (18–36 in), bears clustered heads of sky-blue, five-petalled star-like flowers from early to late summer. There are also pink and white-flowered forms. Both the leaves and the flowers are covered in bristly hairs.

Native to North Africa and central Europe, it is widely found as an escapee from herb gardens – borage has a long history of medicinal and culinary use. It was also introduced into North America where it is widely established.

You'll find it: in well-drained soil with a sunny, warm aspect. It is more abundant in light soils than in heavy ones. Each year it readily grows from self-sown seeds and often forms large colonies, especially around old herb gardens and allotments.

Leaves: oblong to oval dull-green leaves have a corrugated surface covered in rough white hairs. The lower leaves are 10–15 cm (4–6 in) long, but those higher up the plant are half that size.

Harvesting the leaves: pick when young and fresh before they harden, and use as soon as possible.

Using the leaves and flowers: leaves have a flavour reminiscent of cucumber and can be infused to make a refreshing drink. Add both leaves and flowers to salads and fruit cups; the flowers can be candied. Before the introduction of cucumbers, the leaves of borage were used to flavour claret cups (borage is still added to that summer favourite, Pimms). Leaves and stems were added to tankards of ale to introduce coolness and young leaves and shoots were used as a pot-herb during times of scarcity.

Caraway (*Carum carvi*)

This hardy biennial, native to a wide area from Europe to Siberia and naturalized in many other regions throughout the world, is primarily grown for its seeds. Caraway is a hollow-stemmed, much-branched plant with masses of feathery, fern-like, mid-green leaves that impart an aniseed-like flavour.

During early and mid-summer, small green flowers appear in umbrella-like heads at the tops of 60–75 cm (2–2½ ft) high, upright stems on two-year-old plants.

You'll find it: at the edges of old and neglected herb gardens and allotments. It is usually found in sunny positions and light well-drained but moisture-retentive soil.

Seeds: after the small whitish-pink flowers fade, seeds slowly appear. These are about 3 mm (⅛ in) long and mature to a greyish-brown.

Harvesting the seeds: as soon as seeds start to ripen, at the end of early summer and into mid-summer, cut off a few stems from a plant. Remember to leave a few flower heads on the plant to produce seeds that will later fall to the ground and create further plants. Tie several stems together and hang upside down in a large paper bag in a dry, cool, airy place until the seeds are dry and fall off the flower heads. When all seeds have fallen, pass through a sieve to remove fine, dust-like material that may have been attached to them.

Using the seeds: used to flavour cakes, bread and buns (rolls), as well as for adding to salads and cheese dishes. They are also superb for introducing flavour to roast pork and lamb, as well as giving more taste-appeal to sausages and cabbage. Store the seeds in dry, air-tight clean jars; don't forget to add a label as seeds from different species often look similar. Young leaves are especially useful for introducing an aniseed flavour to soups.

Chamomile (*Chamaemelum nobile*)
Also known as: Common Chamomile,
Garden Chamomile, Russian Chamomile

Earlier known as *Anthemis nobilis*, this mat
forming, creeping perennial has been used
instead of grass to create beautifully
aromatic lawns. Nowadays chamomile
lawns are created from the variety
'Treneague', which is non-flowering and
needs little clipping to keep it low and tidy.
The mid-green, finely dissected, somewhat
moss-like aromatic leaves have a fruity scent
when bruised, and yield an essential oil.
   Common Chamomile is native to southern
and western Europe, North Africa and the Azores. It has been
taken to many warm and temperate countries, including North
America, where it has escaped into the countryside.

You'll find it: along roadsides, sandy and well-drained commons
and pastures.
Petals: plants 10–30 cm (4–12 in) high display daisy-like flowers with
white petals and yellow centres, singly on long stems from early to
late summer.
Harvesting the petals: collect flowers when fully open (usually during
mid- and late summer) or when the petals are starting to turn down; use
scissors to snip them off close to the stem's base.
Using the petals: an infusion of 25 g (1 oz) of
flowers to a pint of boiling water makes a
soothing tea. If you want to be able to make
this drink out-of-season, pick the flowers
and dry them on pieces of paper in a warm,
well-ventilated room. When the heads are
papery, place in dry, screw-topped jars; they
keep well for several months.

Wild Chamomile Known
as *Matricaria recutita* or, earlier
as *Matricaria chamomilla*, Wild
Chamomile is an annual with light-
green, finely dissected leaves that
emit an apple-like scent when
bruised. White, daisy-like flowers
appear in mid- and late summer and
can be used in the same way as the
perennial form of Chamomile.

Chervil (*Anthriscus cerefolium*)
Also known as: Salad Chervil

Biennial or annual in nature, this culinary herb is native to the Caucasus, western Asia and southern and central Russia. It is naturalized in many warm and temperate regions in both hemispheres. Growing 30–45 cm (12–18 in), its ridged, hollow stems produce a strongly aniseed aroma when bruised. Note that the highly poisonous Hemlock and Fool's Parsley have similar characteristics to Chervil, so make certain you know what you are gathering.

When growing as a biennial, the plant produces umbrella-like heads, up to 7.5 cm (3 in) across, of white flowers from early to late summer in its second year.

Freezing herbs

Along with other herbs – including parsley, basil, chives and mint – young chervil leaves can be frozen. They retain their flavour, although once thawed are limp and therefore best used for flavouring food, rather than as a garnish. Always choose young, clean and pest- and disease-free leaves for freezing. There are two ways to freeze these types of herbs:
• Pick young leaves, put loosely in freezer bags and seal securely. Place these bags in rigid containers to prevent the leaves being squashed, then place in a freezer.
• Chop up young, clean leaves, place in ice-cube trays and top up with water and freeze. You can then add the frozen cubes directly to food during cooking.
With both freezing methods, all of these herbs are best used within six months of freezing.

You'll find it: around old neglected and abandoned gardens and on hedge banks. It grows well in all soils, in full sunlight or shade.

Leaves: bright green and fern-like, resembling those of parsley. With age they assume deeper shades of green and become tough.

Harvesting the leaves: take only a few leaves at a time from each plant, so that it can continue to make healthy growth.

Using the leaves: use in sandwiches and to garnish and flavour salads, soups, egg and fish dishes. Chervil is a constituent of *fines herbes,* along with parsley, chives and tarragon. Leaves can be dried slowly in slight warmth and used in stuffings.

Chives (*Allium schoenoprasum*)

Also known as: Ail Civitte, Cive, Ezo-negi, Schnittlauch

Hardy, clump-forming, tuft-based perennial with edible leaves. Additionally, during early and mid-summer it has a decorative quality, with bell-shaped lilac flowers crowded in a dense umbel and borne at the tops of upright stems 15–20 cm (6–8 in) high. Chives are found in most of the northern hemisphere and are also widely cultivated as a culinary herb.

You'll find it: because it is clump-forming, after some time in cultivation plants are dug up and divided, with older parts from the centre discarded and young pieces from around the outside replanted. For this reason, it is seen as an escapee around old heaps of soil or on old rubbish heaps where disgarded clumps have been thrown. Look out for it at the edges of allotments or old vegetable gardens.

Leaves: grass-like, tubular and mid-green, with a delicate and mild onion-like flavour.

Harvesting the leaves: rather than tearing from the plant's base, use scissors or a sharp knife to sever as low down as possible. Always choose the younger leaves and do not remove all the stems from one plant.

Using the leaves: their mild onion flavour make the leaves ideal in omelettes, soups, egg and cheese dishes; they also bring extra flavour to sandwiches. Use finely chopped chives as a garnish for mashed (creamed) potatoes, add to small boiled new potatoes, to meat pies and steak puddings.

The leaves can also be used in *fines herbes* and in tartare sauce. It is also a welcome addition to yoghurt-based sauces and dips such as tzatziki. Leaves can be frozen in exactly the same way suggested for Chervil (see page 43). The flowers make a pretty garnish in salads.

> **Herb of legends**
>
> The Romans spread chives throughout much of their empire, believing that it could ease the pain of a sore throat and relieve sunburn. Later, it was claimed that a bunch of dried chives, when hung around a house, warded off evil spirits and diseases.

Coriander (*Coriandrum sativum*)
Also known as: Chinese Parsley, Cilantro

This distinctive culinary herb has erect
stems and a branching nature, together with
fern-like dark-green leaves, and throughout
summer it displays pink-mauve or white flowers
borne in umbrella-like heads. Its height varies,
23–75 cm (9–30 in), and therefore sometimes becomes
lost among other escapees from cultivation. It is a
hardy annual and each year increases itself from seeds.
  An additional quality of this Mediterranean native, now
widely spread and naturalized throughout warm and temperate
climates, is its aromatic, ridged, initially green fruits that enclose
seeds widely used as culinary flavourings.

You'll find it: in bare patches around old herb gardens where
it slowly colonizes large areas – but not densely. It prefers light soil and a
warm and sheltered spot away from cold winds.
Leaves and seeds: leaves have a bug-like scent when young and
especially if bruised, but with age this disappears to reveal a sweet, spicy
fragrance. Similarly, the seeds assume a rich spiciness.
Harvesting leaves and seeds: cut the leaves when young and use
before they wilt and dry. Sever the stems of flower heads when the fruits
have turned from green to grey. Place upside down in paper bags so that
the fruits will be caught and retained and dry slowly in gentle warmth.
Rub to expel the seeds, which can be stored whole or ground to
powder and stored in air-tight glass
jars. Use within a year.
Using the leaves and seeds: the
spicy leaves can be added to broths,
soups and meat dishes, as well as
salads, while the seeds introduce a
distinctive taste to curries and stews.

Aromatic oil The seeds are a
source of an essential oil, which
is used to flavour food, employed
as a carminative and in perfumery
and soap manufacture. The oil is
extracted by steam distillation.

Dill (*Anethum graveolens*)
Also known as: Dillweed

This hardy annual, earlier known as *Peucedanum graveolens*, is widely grown in herb gardens and is often seen as an escapee. Growing 60–90 cm (2–3 ft) high, it has an upright nature with hollow, ridged stems. Native to sunny parts of Europe and southwest Asia, it is now naturalized in many warm regions, including the West Indies, southern parts of North America, Australia and New Zealand. It reproduces itself by self-sown seedlings and as an escapee has colonized many other countries.

You'll find it: around the edges of old and abandoned herb gardens, especially where the soil is light and the position warm and sunny.

Leaves and seeds: the blue-green, thread-like and feathery leaves that appear during summer have a distinctive aniseed flavour. From early to mid-summer it bears small, yellow, star-like flowers in umbrella-like heads about 7.5 cm (3 in) wide. These flowers later produce small, brownish, slightly flattened seeds with thin, yellow ridges.

Harvesting leaves and seeds: cut off young leaves throughout summer, but taking care not to defoliate plants. The leaves are difficult to dry, but can be frozen in the same way as Chervil (page 43). Gather the umbrella-like seed heads when the fruits change from green to brown, and place inside paper bags. They can be gathered and stored in airtight containers, where they keep well for up to a year.

Using leaves and seeds: newly gathered leaves need to be used while still fresh as garnishes and flavouring for fish, boiled potatoes, beans, peas, poultry and soups. They can also be added to salads. Seeds are added to vinegar when making pickles and add a piquancy to sauces.

Dippy Dill Add a tablespoon of finely chopped Dill, a crushed garlic clove and a good grind of black pepper to 250 ml (8 fl oz) plain yoghurt to make a quick summer dip for crudités. Dill also goes remarkably well with poached or grilled salmon.

Fennel (*Foeniculum vulgare*)

Hardy herbaceous perennial native to Mediterranean regions but now naturalized in many warm and temperate climates, where it grows 2 m (7 ft) or more high. It often appears as a haze of finely narrow leaves held on a framework of stiff, upright stems. It is sometimes confused with Dill (page 46), but grows taller, has a perennial nature and finer leaves. It is also somewhat similar to the highly poisonous Hemlock so be certain of what you are gathering.

You'll find it: old herb gardens and allotments, as well as on wasteland, especially if the soil is slightly damp and moisture-retentive. It is also found in coastal areas and among old heaps of soil, where it has become naturalized.

Leaves and seeds: the thread-like, bright green to blue-green aromatic leaves appear in spring or early summer, with golden-yellow flowers packed in 10 cm (4 in) wide umbrella-like heads during mid- and late summer, and sometimes later in warm, mild summers.

Harvesting leaves and seeds: pick young leaves fresh throughout summer, taking care not to decimate plants. Leaves cannot be dried, but freezing is a possibility (see Chervil on page 43 for details). Gather seed heads in late autumn, just before they are fully ripe. Spread seeds on white paper and allow them to dry naturally in gentle warmth. Store in airtight jars for up to a year.

Using leaves and seeds: leaves are used to flavour egg and fish dishes, as well as in risottos, salads and with vegetables. The strongly aniseed-flavoured seeds are added to breads, cakes and soups and to Italian sausages and meatballs. The seeds are also widely used to make an effective digestive tea.

Confusing namesake Apart from Fennel, there is Florence Fennel, sometimes known as Finocchio and botanically as *Foeniculum vulgare* var. *dulce*. It grows as an annual, has a similar but shorter appearance to Fennel and a bulbous base to its stem. These stem-bases have a sweet, anise-like flavour and are used raw in salads and cooked as a vegetable. Alternatively, they can be braised in stock to add further flavour.

Horseradish (*Armoracia rusticana*)
Also known as: Great Railfort, Mountain Radish, Red Cole

Earlier known as *Cochlearia armoracia*, this popular hardy herbaceous perennial is famed for its pungently flavoured roots. Its large rough surfaced, dark green, dock-like leaves have lobed or wavy edges and grow to about 45 cm (18 in) long. Small white cross-shaped flowers appear from late spring to late summer on long stems often hidden among the leaves. But it is the thick main root, often 25 cm (10 in) or more deep, that is the reason this plant is grown.

Native to southeast Europe and western Asia, it has become naturalized as an escapee in both hemispheres, and is widespread in North America.

You'll find it: around abandoned and derelict gardens, allotments and rubbish heaps. When in cultivation it is increased by dividing roots, parts are abandoned and these often colonize areas around gardens. Before digging up roots of plants growing in the wild, the law indicates that you will need permission from the land owner.

Roots: the long, thick, yellowish-buff roots have a distinctive and pungent peppery aroma and taste.

Harvesting the roots: look for plants at the edges of clumps and use a spade to remove them. Roots in light, sandy soil are much easier to dig up than branching ones in heavy soils. Wash, allow to dry and store in dry sand or peat in a cool dark shed, cellar or garage. They remain in good condition for several months.

Using the roots: peel the root, ensuring the brown layer under the surface is removed. This preparation is best undertaken under a running tap or in a bowl of water as it reduces the pungency of the root. The root can then be grated, minced or crushed and simmered with milk and seasonings to make a peppery sauce to flavour meat, fish and salads. Horseradish sauce is widely used with roast beef. Freshly grated roots can be used as a garnish for beef or smoked fish such as mackerel.

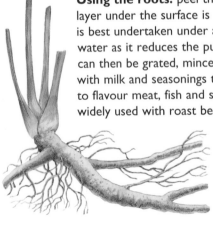

MINTS: Peppermint (*Mentha* x *piperita*)
Also known as: Spanish or Corsican Mint

This hardy herbaceous perennial grows to 30–80 cm (1½–2½ ft) high, with masses of lilac-pink to light purple flowers appearing in long clustered heads during summer. It is a natural hybrid between Water Mint (*M. aquatica*) and Spearmint (*M. spicata*).

You'll find it: older parts from the plant's centre when being divided are often discarded around rubbish and soil heaps where they establish themselves. Look alongside allotments and old herb gardens. As an escapee, it is also found in ditches, along roadsides and in waste areas.
Leaves: lance-shaped to oval, hairy, mid-green and tooth edged on short stalks, the leaves are sometimes reddish green. Leaves have a strong peppermint aroma and flavour.
Harvesting the leaves: pick young leaves in spring and summer and use as fresh as possible.
Using the leaves: add sprigs of young leaves to cool summer drinks and to flavour vegetables. The flavour of new potatoes and peas is greatly enhanced by a few sprigs added to the cooking water. Remove the sprigs before serving. When infused, Peppermint makes a refreshing tea.

Other peppermints: The prostrate and carpeting *M. requienii* is also known as Peppermint, as well as being called Spanish Mint, Corsican Mint and Corsican Thyme. It has round, bright, pale green leaves that when bruised have a distinctive peppermint scent. Throughout the summer it bears long spikes of pale purple flowers and is sometimes grown in combination with Thyme and Chamomile to form a fragrant lawn.

MINTS: Water Mint (*Mentha aquatica*)

Another member of the mint family, this strongly scented perennial herb is native throughout Europe, parts of Asia and Africa. It has also spread to many temperate countries.

Its small lilac flowers are densely crowded into terminal heads and borne on branched, square stems from early summer to early autumn.

You'll find it: alongside streams, rivers and ponds, as well as in damp meadows, marshes and fens, where it grows in clumps about 60 cm (2 ft) high.

Leaves: somewhat rough surfaced, oval and hairy dark green leaves with purple tinges.

Harvesting the leaves: gather leaves from the top and outside of a clump since these will be more tender and less bitter than more mature leaves.

Using the leaves: Use in the same way as for Peppermint and other mints to make sauces, chutneys, cold drinks and tea infusions, although you might find the taste slightly bitter. In this case, add sugar to sweeten.

Other mints to consider

- **Ginger Mint** (*Mentha* x *gracilis*) has yellow variegations to the bright green leaves and a ginger-like scent when bruised.
- **Apple mint** (*Mentha suaveolens*) sometimes called Woolly Mint, has light green leaves and light purple to pink flowers. It is used to make Apple Mint jelly and added to salads and drinks.
- **Pineapple Mint** (*Mentha suaveolens* 'Variegata') has leaves with creamy-white edges and a pineapple aroma.
- **Spearmint** (*Mentha spicata*) or Common Mint is a hardy herbaceous, clump-forming perennial that has a large mass of spearmint-flavoured leaves. It bears pale-purple flowers in dense whorls along branching stems, which grow 45–60 cm (1½–2 ft) high, from mid-summer to early autumn. Native to southern and central Europe, it now grows in temperate climates throughout the world; in many areas it has escaped from cultivation and into the countryside. It is often found in old and neglected cottage gardens, the edges of allotments and country lanes. It is often grown in large tins and pots to constrict growth and prevent its spread.

Rosemary (*Rosmarinus officinalis*)

Native to Mediterranean countries and southern Turkey, this evergreen aromatic shrub now grows in many warm and temperate regions throughout the world. In earlier years it was especially planted at the fronts of cottages to confirm its legend as the herb of remembrance.

Growing 1.5–2 m (5–7 ft) high, it spreads and eventually colonizes large areas; its self-sown seeds ensure its spread. During mid- and late spring – and sporadically through to late summer and sometimes into early winter – it bears mauve tubular flowers with prominent lower lips; the flowers cluster in leaf joints.

You'll find it: alongside country lanes and near old cottages; additionally, in old and neglected herb gardens and especially where plants were discarded in warm and sheltered corners.

Leaves: narrow, mid- to dark green and clustered around stems that are mainly upright but in old plants fall sideways and almost rest on the ground.

Harvesting the leaves: carefully pull off leaves by snapping them sideways; they can be used fresh or dried. To dry them, cut off whole stems and hang them upside-down in a cool room. Unfortunately, dried leaves lose some flavour.

Using the leaves: they are used fresh or dried to introduce further flavour to lamb, pork and veal. Rosemary is also superb for flavouring poultry dishes, roasted vegetables, eggs and fish as well as sauces and stuffings.

Uses for Rosemary

• When making roast potatoes, add a scattering of fresh or dried Rosemary leaves to the hot oil in your roasting pan. Shake the pan gently to coat the potatoes with the Rosemary and the oil. Season with salt and roast as normal.

• A sprig of Rosemary in any tomato-based sauce adds a Mediterranean twist.

• It makes a flavourful contribution to minestrone and other vegetable soups and stews.

• Stuff sprigs of Rosemary into the cavity of whole fish or chicken before roasting or barbecuing.

Summer Savory (*Satureja hortensis*)

Summer Savory has an annual nature and forms a mass of young stems, growing 30–45 cm (30–18 in) high. It is native to southern Europe but has spread to many temperate countries, where it escapes and each year produces seeds that perpetuate it.

You'll find it: around old herb gardens and allotments, and especially in disused country gardens. Also look for it on old heaps of soil close to retired herb gardens, where it might have been discarded and formed seed-raised colonies.

Leaves: Spicily flavoured, dark green leaves are borne on square, hairy stems. From mid-summer to early autumn, stems becomes covered in tiny, tubular, lilac flowers that arise from leaf joints.

Harvesting the leaves: pick young leaves throughout summer and use fresh. Apart from using them soon after being gathered, leaves can be dried for winter use. This is best done by cutting down plants at the end of summer, tying them in bunches and hanging them upside-down in a dry, cool and airy place. Leaves can be removed as they are required.

Using the leaves: to flavour fish and meat, as well as soups, cheese and egg dishes, drinks and stuffings. In southern Europe, Summer Savory is often used when cooking broad (fava) beans.

Winter Savory (*Satureja montana*)

A hardy perennial with a bushy, erect and woody sub-shrub nature, Winter Savory grows up to 30 cm (12 in) high, sometimes slightly more. From mid-summer to mid-autumn it bears rose-purple, tubular-shaped flowers from the upper leaf joints.

Native to southern Europe and parts of North Africa, it is popular in herb gardens, from where it is often an escapee. In warmer areas it sometimes becomes naturalized on old stone walls.

It has square-sectioned stems bearing grey-green, narrow or lance-shaped leaves. It is characterized by having a series of small but visible ridges around each stem and between pairs of leaves.

The flavour is considered to be coarser than leaves from Summer Savory (see above).

Tansy (*Tanacetum vulgare*)

Also known as: Bitter Buttons, Common Tansy, Cow Bitter, Garden Tansy, Golden Buttons

A widespread and popular herb with an herbaceous and perennial nature, Tansy is native to Europe and Asia, including Siberia, and has been introduced into North America and countries in the southern hemisphere. It is now naturalized throughout warm and temperate climates.

With its traditional culinary, medicinal and domestic uses, this cottage-garden perennial was widely grown in herb and kitchen gardens, where it created a dominant display of leaves and flowers. It grows to 1 m (3½ ft) high, sometimes more.

You'll find it: old and grassy areas as well as alongside fields, roadsides, hedgerows, country paths, old gardens and allotments. It is especially found in areas where old cottages have been demolished or abandoned.

Leaves and flowers: erect stems bear large, deeply divided, dark green leaves with serrated edges. Bright, golden-yellow, button-like flowers appear in clustered heads from mid- to late summer.

Harvesting the leaves and young shoots: use a sharp knife to cut off young leaves; old ones are too tough. Also cut off tender young shoots.

Using the leaves and shoots: young leaves and shoots can be used to flavour omelettes; if shredded, they can be added to sandwiches and cheese dishes. Leaves have also been used in traditional puddings and cakes, such as Easter Tansy Pudding. Young leaves were served with fried eggs.

Tansy tea was popular and was also used as a tonic, a stimulant and for treating children who had worms.

Popular strewing herb Several centuries ago, many aromatic herbs were strewn on floors of churches, castles and baronial halls to create a fragrant atmosphere. Tansy, with its distinctive but not particularly appealing scent of chest ointment, was widely used and reputed to keep away flies and to deter lice and fleas. When combined with elder leaves it was especially protective against flies and moths. However, a more fragrant combination is Tansy leaves, Rosemary and Thyme.

Wild Garlic (*Allium ursinum*)

Also known as: Ramsons, Wood Garlic, Bear's Garlic, Buckrams, Devil's Posy, Gypsy Garlic, Hog Garlic, Gypsy Gibbles

A bulbous-based herbaceous perennial with a clump-forming then carpeting nature, it displays umbrella-like heads of 6 to 20 white star-like flowers from mid-spring to early summer, rising above the leaves that grow 50 cm (20 in) high. Native to large parts of Europe, Scandinavia, central Russia and from Spain to the Caucasus and southern Turkey, it also flourishes in North America where it was introduced.

You'll find it: in damp woods and shady places. Note that it is similar to the poisonous lily-of-the-valley before it flowers. Crush a leaf in your fingers to determine which it is – the garlic scent is an indication that you have found an edible plant.

Leaves: bright green, flat and broadly lance-shaped leaves about 20 cm (8 in) long are supported on stiff triangular stems and have a distinctive garlic scent.

Harvesting the leaves: choose young and fresh leaves as these have the best flavour. Although animals usually avoid this plant, it is always best to wash before eating them.

Using the leaves: although collectively they create a strong garlic aroma, individually and when added to salads their impact is much less. Use as a cooked vegetable or in any recipe calling for garlic, it can also be added to risottos and soups, and makes a very good pesto.

Garlic In warm regions, especially if the soil is light and well-drained, you might find escapees of the bulbous-based culinary herb *Allium sativum*, native of Central Asia. Used to flavour many foods including salads, fish and meat dishes, it is common in the cuisines of many diverse cultures, from French, Italian and Polish to Chinese, Thai and West Indian.

Wild Marjoram (*Origanum vulgare*)
Also known as: Common Marjoram, Oregano, Organy, Herb Oregano

With a perennial nature, but also spreading by seeds, Wild Marjoram grows 30–60 cm (1–2 ft) high, sometimes slightly more. Native to southern Europe and northern and western Asia, it has spread to many temperate countries and regions.

You'll find it: dry, hilly pastures and banks, alongside roads and paths and especially where soil is chalky.

Leaves and flowers: tiny, tubular, rose-purple flowers, borne in densely clustered heads at the tops of stems during mid- and late summer. The round to oval green, grey-tinted leaves are nearly stalkless and appear on branched stems.

Harvesting the leaves: cut off a few sprigs of young leaves, but do not decimate plants.

Using the leaves: can be used fresh or gently dried slowly in the sun, when they become sweeter. It is an ideal wayside herb for flavouring meat dishes, stews and casseroles.

Other Marjorams

You might find other Marjorams that have escaped from herb gardens including:
- Knotted Marjoram (*Origanum majorana*) also known as Annual Marjoram and Sweet Marjoram, is a tender perennial growing annually from seeds with a shrubby and bushy nature. Bright green leaves develop from knot-like leaf joints that cluster around red, four-sided stems. Clusters of white, pink or mauve flowers appear from early to late summer. Young leaves and shoots are used to flavour meat or poultry, as well as in stuffings. Leaves have a stronger flavour when dried and are often used in *pot-pourri*. It is also a traditional part of *bouquet garni*.
- Pot Marjoram (*Origanum onites*) is a perennial, shrub-like and sprawling plant with bright green, aromatic leaves. It is usually raised annually from seeds and therefore spreads when seeds scatter or plants are discarded at the end of summer. Its branching nature and reddish tinge to the entire plant make it noticeable. Use young leaves, fresh or dried, in stuffings and to flavour meat, poultry, soups, omelettes and sausagemeat. It is also popular with veal.

Wild fruits

The strict botanic definition of fruits encompasses nuts as well as the soft and fleshy wayside fruits such as blackberries, cranberries and wild strawberries. However, this chapter is devoted to the juicy succulent fruits and the next chapter deals with nuts.

These much-desired fruits are borne on a wide range of plants, from ground-hugging evergreen shrubs to brambles with long, thorny stems and trees providing fruits such as elderberries, hawthorns and sloes.

Knowing where and when to search for country fruits is a major element in successful foraging, especially as many provide easy pickings for native animals and birds. For each of the fruits in this chapter, the timing and where to find it are clearly indicated, since this is crucial to foraging success.

Do not expect to gather masses of these fruits at one time since, within even a small area, fruits differ in their ripening and picking times. Most are picked and eaten as treats, but where foraging brings in several bowlfuls of the same type of fruit, then jams, jellies, sauces, and pies are possible.

After spending hours searching out and picking wayside fruits, the last thing you want to do is to knock over the container. Always pick fruits into flat-based boxes and regularly tip them into a larger container that has a lid. This way, even if you knock over the picking box you will not lose your complete harvest.

Thoroughly cleaned large plastic ice-cream containers are ideal when foraging as the lids can be snapped open and closed very easily. They can be labelled with a permanent marker-pen if you are foraging for several different fruits at one time.

If you arrive home from foraging with no telltale signs on your fingers and lips of eating a few (or more) fruits along the way, then you will not have enjoyed yourself to the full!

Barberry (*Berberis vulgaris*)

Also known as: Common Barberry, Jaundice Berry, Pipperidge, Piprage

You might see this thorny, deciduous shrub in old and neglected gardens where it was once grown for its 5–7.5 cm (2–3 in) long pendulous clusters of yellow flowers, followed by red berries.

It is native to large parts of Europe, northern Africa and temperate Asia, as well as abundant and now naturalized in North America where it was introduced by early settlers.

You'll find it: in old gardens it was traditionally used as a hedging plant, so do not be surprised if you find it around abandoned buildings and alongside roads. Also look for it on wasteland around old dwellings.

Fruits: red oblong berries, 12 mm (½ in) long, appear in late summer. These are high in vitamin C and are an important food for small birds. Barberry has also been used to treat liver complaints and jaundice in alternative medicine. However, its very sharp thorns make it quite difficult to pick the fruits in some locations.

Harvesting the fruits: berries are ripe enough to be picked in autumn when they turn a deep red. Use gloves as the prickly stems can damage your fingers and hands.

Using the fruits: although acidic, they can be eaten raw and are considered a delicacy in some cultures. However, they are more palatable when candied or preserved in sugar. The fruits make good jams and jellies – use the recipe for Hawthorn jelly (see page 71) as a template for making Barberry jelly. In eastern Europe this jelly is traditionally used to accompany roast meats.

Iranian delicacy The dried fruit of Barberry is widely used in Iranian cooking – Iran is the world's largest producer of dried Barberry, known as *zereshk* in Persian. *Zereshk* is added to chicken dishes to give a tart flavour, and is also cooked in rice, made into jams, juices and fruit rolls in Iran. Try adding a few fresh or dried berries to rice during cooking to give a sharp note to the dish.

Bilberry (*Vaccinium myrtillus*)

Also known as: Blaeberry, Crowberry, Whinberry, Whortleberry

Few plants have such delicious fruits as this hardy, deciduous, spreading shrub. Native to large parts of central and northern Europe, its appearance belies its value as a foraging plant. Earlier it was widely planted in North America, where it is now established.

Growing 30–60 cm (1–2 ft) high, it is smothered in oval, slightly pointed and finely tooth-edged, bright green leaves. Drooping, greenish-pink rounded flowers are borne singly or in pairs in terminal and side clusters during late spring.

You'll find it: abundant on mountainsides, in open woodland and on acid heaths and moors. In windswept areas you need to search carefully for this plant, as it grows lower than usual.
Fruits: round, juicy bluish-black and 6 mm (¼ in) across. They often cluster under leaves and unless searched out are not easily seen.
Harvesting the fruits: berries are ready for picking from mid-summer to early autumn.

Using the fruits: wash before eating. Large fruits are superb with sugar and cream. They make tasty tarts and jams, and can be added to stewed fruits. The dried leaves can be infused in boiling water to make a tea substitute.

Bilberry tart

There are numerous recipes for Bilberry tart but the following one has proved to be popular.

- 1½ teacups of large, washed bilberries
- 4 tbsp caster (superfine) sugar
- 20 cm (8 in) wide tart tin lined with sweet short-crust pastry. Bake blind to create a base for the berries.
- 4 egg yolks
- 4 tbsp double cream
- 6 fresh bay leaves

Heat the oven to 180°C (350°F/gas mark 4). Mix together the sugar and bilberries and tip into the prepared tart case. Beat together the egg yolks and cream, then pour the mixture over the sugared berries. Place bay leaves on top of the tart and bake for 25 minutes or until set. Eat warm or at room temperature. A dollop of cream or vanilla ice cream are delicious companions to this tart!

Blackberry (*Rubus fruticosus*)
Also known as: Bramble, Brier

Perhaps one of the best-known foraging plants, with lusciously sweet berries in late summer and autumn. The green, prickly, bramble-like leaves assume reddish-purple shades in autumn. During early and mid-summer, white or pink flowers, about 30 mm (1 in) wide, appear in clusters. Later, these are the source of the fruits.

Native to Europe (especially southern regions), Mediterranean regions and Macaronesia (islands in the North Atlantic ocean, including the Azores, Canary Islands, Cape Verde, and Madeira) but widely naturalized around the temperate regions.

Blackberry sauce

This is an easy recipe and is excellent with duck, pork or turkey.

- 450 g (1 lb) blackberries
- 3 tbsp caster (superfine) sugar
- 1 tbsp lemon juice

Mix the blackberries, sugar and lemon juice in a saucepan.

Cover and simmer gently for about ten minutes.

Remove from the heat, allow to cool slightly, and then blend in a food processer or blender.

Strain the mixture to remove seeds and pour into sterilized glass jars. Seal and label the jars when cool. The sauce can be kept in a refrigerator for two or three months, but is best used soon after making.

You'll find it: widespread in hedges and woods, alongside roads and in old, neglected gardens and allotments, where it forms a tangle of near impenetrable, thorny, arching stems.

Fruits: colour changes from green to red before finally turning rich purple when they are ready for picking.

Harvesting the fruits: place the fruits in shallow punnets and avoid squashing. Try not to collect more fruits than you can eat; leave some for the wildlife.

Using the fruits: most fruits are eaten fresh, sometimes with a dusting of sugar and cream, but such is the versatility of black-berries that they are used in a wide range of desserts and jams. They are particularly good with apples in a crumble, in blackberry fool and pancakes, and of course, with vanilla ice cream.

Blackcurrant (*Ribes nigrum*)
Also known as: European Black Currant, Squinancy Berry

Widely grown in gardens, it is native to much of Europe as well as north and central Asia to the Himalayas. This hardy clump-forming shrub, up to 1.5 m (5 ft) high, has large, matt green, three- or five-lobed leaves. It bears clusters of drooping, dull purplish-green flowers, followed by sprigs of round berries that ripen in the latter part of mid-summer.

You'll find it: in moisture-retentive soil in woods and alongside banks.

Fruits: distinctively black and glossy, but not in such large and dense clusters as cultivated blackcurrants.

Harvesting the fruits: pick entire sprigs (clusters) of the fruits, not individual berries. When you get them home, remove individual berries from stalks and place in a cool larder rather than the refrigerator since they lose some flavour if excessively chilled.

Using the fruits: apart from being used fresh with a dusting of sugar and cream, they are made into jams and put in flans and pies. They are also superb in muffins, fools and as toppings for cheesecake and ice creams. Blackcurrants have been the source of an extremely popular juice and are very high in vitamin C.

Sore throat remedy
Blackcurrants have been gathered in the wild for many centuries before the plant began to be cultivated in gardens. The fruits were used in folk medicine to alleviate a sore throat, known as a quinsy and this led to the plant being called Squinancy, an earlier but still relevant common name. Its effectiveness for easing sore throats was vindicated during the Second World War (1939–45) when commercially bottled blackcurrant syrup was given to children suffering from that complaint.

Tea tricks
Transform a pot of ordinary Indian tea, and give it the flavour of green tea from China by adding dried blackcurrant leaves to the infusion. When fresh, Blackcurrant leaves have a heavy, aromatic aroma, especially when crushed.

Bullace (*Prunus domestica* subsp. *insititia*)
Also known as: Bullace Plum, Bullums, Bullison, Damson Plum, Green Damson

Closely related to Damsons, the Bullace is sometimes classified as *Prunus insititia*. It is deciduous, brown-barked and usually forms a densely twiggy and thorny shrub, although it can reach tree-like stature of 1.8–4.5 m (6–15 ft) high.

Its hairy surfaced leaves are long, dull greyish green and coarsely tooth-edged. It flowers during mid- and late spring, with pear-shaped, broad, pure white petals.

It is a natural hybrid and was widely cultivated in Europe and southwest Asia but later became neglected when improved plum varieties were developed. It was introduced into North America and became known as Bullace Plum and Damson Plum.

You'll find it: usually near old and abandoned orchards, in hedges, old gardens and undisturbed corners. It is often found in areas quite remote from houses.

Fruits: round or shortly oval drooping fruits are usually blue-black and with a white bloom, or purple. They are 18–25 mm (¾–1 in) wide and larger than the fruits of Sloes (see page 81). The stone is bluntly angled, with the fruit's soft flesh clinging to it.

Harvesting the fruits: although more palatable than the fruits of sloes, their taste is so sharp that they are often left on the shrub or tree until mid- or late autumn. This enables early frosts to soften the flesh and decrease their acidity.

Using the fruits: the range of uses for Bullaces is wide and certainly in earlier years it was an important culinary fruit in autumn. However, as new varieties of plums, damsons and gages were introduced, its importance faded. Nevertheless, as a foraging fruit it is worth seeking, with uses ranging from jams and sauces (especially to accompany wood pigeon) and to make Bullace vodka (see page 81 and adapt the recipe for Sloe gin using vodka or gin if you prefer).

Cherry Plum (*Prunus cerasifera*)
Also known as: Myrobalan Plum

This deciduous spreading tree can grow 8 m
(26 ft) tall in the wild but it is mostly found as a
scrambling hedgerow plant. It has finely toothed
oval, alternate leaves and white flowers with five
petals that open before the leaves in early spring.
Since it is the first Prunus to flower, it is often
confused with Sloe (see page 81).
   Native to a wide range of areas in Europe and
Asia, it has been widely cultivated and has become
naturalized in North America.

You'll find it: especially alongside hedgerows and
thickets on all but the poorest soil. Since it has been
widely cultivated, look for it in old and neglected gardens
and old orchards. It has also been grown as a decorative
shrub and tree.
Fruits: round 2–3 cm (1–1¼ in) across with a stone, the fruits can be
either red or yellow. Some foragers claim the taste is a combination of
cherry and plum. They can be eaten fresh but some are quite dry and may
need to be transformed into preserves or jellies.
Harvesting the fruits: ripening from mid-summer to early autumn,
try to harvest before the birds get to them. Cut them off and either eat
immediately or store in shallow boxes in a well ventilated room. Use as
soon as possible.
Using the fruits: they can be eaten immediately when ripe and on
picking. To many tastes they are sharp, but make excellent jams, jellies and
chutney. Try Cherry Plums in a summer fruit cobbler with other foraged
fruits such as blackberries or raspberries.

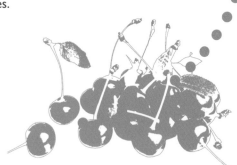

Cloudberry (*Rubus chamaemorus*)

Also known as: Baked Apple, Baked Apple Berry, Malka, Salmonberry, Yellow Berry

Hardy low-growing herbaceous perennial, usually only 7.5–25 cm (3–10 in) high, depending on the barrenness of the area, with a creeping rootstock that enables it to survive cold regions. Sometimes it has an annual nature and increases itself by seeds each year.

It is native to a wide area of the northern hemisphere, including North America, northern Europe, Scandinavia and Arctic Russia to central Russia and Germany. Plants flower from early to late summer, with five-petalled white flowers that are highly attractive to flies and bumble bees. Some plants are male, others female: each plant usually has just one flower, with only female plants producing berries.

You'll find it: on open moorland and mountains, and growing among other plants, including heather, cotton grass and mosses.

Fruits: at first red and clustering in groups at the tops of stems, they become yellow or amber when ripe during late summer and early autumn. They are often described as small, orange globules packed in heads shaped like a raspberry.

Harvesting the fruits: this needs to be done as soon as the berries ripen, as insects find them tasty. It is a back-breaking task, searching the ground low down and this accounts for the high cost when buying them.

Using the fruits: they are especially tasty when eaten fresh with vanilla ice cream. Foragers new to these berries often find the seeds tough and therefore boil the entire fruits, adding sugar to make jam. This mixture can be reprocessed to make jellies and juices, blended with chocolate ice cream, or made into a refreshing and unique marmalade.

Cowberry (*Vaccinium vitis-idaea*)
Also known as: Clusterberry, Crowberry, Foxberry,
Lingonberry, Mountain Cranberry, Quailberry,
Red Whortleberry

This hardy evergreen shrub with creeping
roots is native to a wide area in the northern
hemisphere, as well as to areas further south
but at high altitudes. It is a popular native plant in
North America where it is cultivated for its berries.
 It rarely grows more than 20 cm (8 in) high, but in
places where the weather is congenial it is slightly more
vigorous – up to 30 cm (12 in). Its dark lustrous green leaves
are oval to pear-shaped, tough with serrated edges. Pink or
white bell-shaped flowers appear in terminal clusters during
late spring and early summer.

You'll find it: on moors and in woods, where the soil
is acidic. It is not easy to find, but often forms large,
if sparse colonies.
Fruits: acidic, globular red berries appear from late
summer to mid-autumn.
Harvesting the fruits: gather the berries as soon as they are red – not
before. Take care not to squash them and get them home as soon as
possible, before they become warm. Place in a cool, airy cupboard, where
they can remain for several weeks.
Using the fruits: often scarcely edible when picked and therefore
usually turned into jams and jellies. However, there are other ways to use
Cowberries: try them in muffins, baked with apples or into buns. They
can also be cooked with cabbage to give a sharp piquancy to a sometimes
dull vegetable. Like Cranberries, Cowberry jelly is particularly good with
turkey, game birds and venison.

Crab apple (*Malus sylvestris*)
Also known as: Crab, Wild Crab Apple, European Apple, Sour Grabs

A native of Europe and southwest Asia and, when introduced into North America, became a widespread escapee. It forms a small tree, up to 7.5 m (25 ft) high, with dull to mid-green leaves, smooth-surfaced and with bluntly toothed edges. It should not be confused with seedlings from orchard apples, which can be distinguished from the wild Crab apple by their downy stems and sweet fruits. During late spring it produces clusters white flowers flushed with pink.

You'll find it: in hedges, woods and scrubland.
Fruits: the round, 18–25 mm (¾–1 in) wide fruits are hard and sour-tasting, greenish-yellow and when ripe, often speckled or flushed with red. Each fruit has a depression at both ends.
Harvesting the fruits: usually ready in late summer or early autumn, when they turn red, start to fall from the tree or their stalks are easily parted from the tree.
Using the fruits: crab apple jelly is perhaps the best known way to use the fruits, but they are also used to make wine, chutney, apple butter and many jelly variations. Try adding two or three crab apples to ordinary apple tarts or crumbles to introduce a sharp note.

Crab Apple Jelly

- 900 g (2 lb) crab apples
- caster (superfine) sugar
- 2 cloves

Chop the apples roughly and put into a preserving pan with cloves and enough water to cover.
Bring to the boil and simmer until soft and pulpy. Skim foam that arises.
Put pulp in muslin layers or a jelly bag to drain overnight, catching the juices in a pan.
Discard the pulp and measure the juice. For every 600 ml (1 pint) of juice add 450 g (1 lb) sugar.
Return juice and sugar to the pan and dissolve sugar by heating gently, then boil rapidly for 20 minutes or until setting point is reached.
Pour into warm sterilized jars and seal while still warm.

Cranberry (*Vaccinium oxycoccos*)

Also known as: **Bog Berry, Small Cranberry**

You might find this hardy, prostrate, evergreen shrub listed as *Oxycoccus palustris*. It is native to a large area from Europe to Scandinavia, central France, northern Italy, northern Asia to Japan, Greenland and many parts of North America.

It has wiry stems and small, oval and pointed, dark green leaves (whitish below); long stems often develop roots which help secure the plant in the ground. Pink flowers, with four spreading or turned-down petals, appear from early to late summer, with the fruits in autumn.

You'll find it: in bogs and wet heaths, but you may need to search for it under other shrubs.

Fruits: round or slightly oval red berries appear from late summer to mid-autumn. Sometimes, they have small, brown spots. The berries are borne individually at the ends of thin stems, which arise from leaf joints along main stems.

Harvesting the fruits: pick the berries individually when richly coloured. Usually, you will not be able to find sufficient berries to make a pie; they are best used to make sauces.

Using the fruits: when picked they have a tart, acidic flavour and to many people's taste are almost inedible when uncooked. Cranberries are at their best when used to make traditional sauces to accompany turkey or venison.

North American introduction
Known as the Large Cranberry or American Cranberry, *Vaccinium macrocarpon* (earlier listed as *Oxycoccus macrocarpos*), is native to North America as well as being introduced into other countries. It has been cultivated in its native countries and Europe for its large berries. It is now ideal for foraging in commercially abandoned areas, and the berries mix very well with smaller-berried species.

Dewberry (*Rubus caesius*)
Also known as: Token Berry, European Dewberry

A popular wild bramble with slender, prickly, sprawling stems, and due to its low, deciduous nature is often unnoticed, especially as it does not produce many fruits during some seasons. This reluctance to bear fruits has encouraged its country name Token Berry. It rarely grows beyond 40 cm (16 in) high. The leaves have three green leaflets, and are slightly hairy on both sides.

Clusters of white, five-petalled flowers appear from early summer to early autumn and are followed by the distinctive fruits. Dewberry is common in many areas particularly along coastal regions in Europe from Scandinavia to Spain, Greece and Sicily, and also in Asia and Russia.

You'll find it: along roadsides, coastal regions, in scrub and dry grassland, and especially in chalky areas. It tends to grow well among blackberries (see page 60).

Fruits: they are different from other bramble fruits in being formed of fewer but larger druplets (individually they form the characteristic clustered shape of fruits in the bramble family). When ripe they are bluish, with a distinctive whitish-bloom.

Dewberry plants often grow in the same areas as blackberries, but they flower earlier and the fruits can be readily identified by their shape and early appearance.

Harvesting the fruits: the fruits are ready for picking from mid-summer to autumn. At this stage they are soft, juicy and easily squashed. For this reason, cut them off in clusters, with a small stem intact and attached to them.

Using the fruits: there are never enough fruits to meet the demand so view dewberries as 'treats'. Eat as you pick or if you manage to get them home, dip using their stems into bowls of cream and sugar.

Elderberry (*Sambucus nigra*)

Also known as: Bour Tree, Common Elder, European Elder

This deciduous shrub or tree, up to 9 m (30 ft) high, is best known for its fragrant flowers and for the dark purplish-red fruits. Native to wide areas of Europe, southwest Asia and northern Africa, it often grows where little else thrives. It has been introduced to many temperate countries, including North America.

Sweet-smelling, creamy-white flowers appear in large, flat heads up to 20 cm (8 in) wide in early summer. The matt-green leaves, usually formed of five leaflets, have an acrid aroma when young.

You'll find it: abundant in woods, waste areas and hedgerows, especially where soil is fertile and moisture-retentive.

Fruits: round berries, first green, then purplish-black and 6 mm (¼ in) wide when ripe, appear in late summer and early autumn.

Harvesting flowers and fruits: cut flowers off in clusters and before using the flowers, check that they are free from insects (shake but don't wash). When ripe, cut off berries in clusters, with a small piece of stem still attached.

Using the fruits and flowers: Elderberry wine can be made from the ripe fruits while the flowers yield that great summer favourite, Elderflower cordial. The fresh flowerheads can also be dipped in a sweet batter and turned into fritters.

Elderflower cordial

- 1.5 kg (3 lb 5 oz) sugar
- 1.2 litres (2 pts) water
- 20 heads elderflowers
- 2 lemons
- 75 g (3 oz) citric acid (available from chemists/pharmacies)

Dissolve the sugar and water in a pan and bring to the boil. Place the flowers in a large bowl. Pare the lemons in wide strips and slice the lemons. Add peel and slices to bowl. Pour over the boiling syrup, stir in the citric acid to dissolve, then cover and let stand overnight. Strain cordial through muslin cloth and place in sterilized screwtop jars or bottles. To use, dilute the cordial with either still or sparkling water

Gooseberry (*Ribes uva-crispa*)
Also known as: English Gooseberry, European Gooseberry, Goosegog

Earlier known as *Ribes grossularia*, this deciduous, spiny, much-branched shrub is native to a wide area, from southern Europe to Scandinavia, and north Africa. It is also established in North America, where it has escaped from cultivation.

Bushes grow about 1 m (3½ ft) high, with three- or five-lobed, matt green leaves and clusters of small, green to pinkish-green flowers with purple tinges during late spring and early summer.

You'll find it: indigenous plants are most often seen in shaded, moisture-retentive areas alongside streams, but escapees from cultivation are found mainly alongside hedges and in woods, where they have been spread by birds eating the fruits and scattering seeds.

Fruits: usually hairy, round or oval, green, yellowish-green or reddish-purple fruits in mid- and late summer borne in small, drooping clusters.

Harvesting the fruits: pick the berries individually as they ripen, leaving the short stalk intact with the fruit. Do not just tear them off the bush. Take care that thorns on the bush do not damage your fingers.

Using the fruits: unripe fruits are sometimes picked early and used with Fennel in a sauce to accompany mackerel. Most fruits, however, are picked when ripe and eaten fresh with a dusting of sugar and cream. They are also ideal in preserves.

As a dessert, gooseberry fool has few rivals and is very easy to make. Simply wash the fruits, then top and tail to remove ends and stems. Simmer 350 g (12 oz) gooseberries in a dash of water and about 85 g (3 oz) sugar (or to taste) for a short time until pulpy and hot. You can then purée the gooseberries in a food processor and seive, or simply crush with a wooden spoon. Allow the purée to cool before folding it into 350 ml (12 fl oz) cold custard or a mix of custard and whipped cream for a delightful summer treat. If you have more or less fruit to start with, then alter the quantities to fit your own situation.

Hawthorn (*Crataegus monogyna*)

Also known as: Common Hawthorn, English Hawthorn,
May-bush, May-tree, Whitethorn, May

A widely seen, spiny-branched, deciduous shrub
or small tree up to 6 m (30 ft) high with shiny dark
green deeply lobed leaves appearing in mid-spring.
These are followed in late spring and early summer by
white (sometimes pink), heavily scented flowers borne
in dense, flattened clusters. Hawthorn is native to wide
areas of Europe and the Mediterranean region to Afghanistan.

You'll find it: in woods and open land, on scrub land and in
country hedges, where it has
been planted for hundreds of
years. Found on most soils,
other than excessively wet land,
fens and bogs.
Fruits: often known as haws,
the deep red round fruits appear
in autumn.
Harvesting the fruits: the
fruits, when glossy and fully ripe,
are best picked in a cluster, taking
care to avoid the prickles. Remove
individually from the group and
wash and dry them.
Using the fruits and leaves:
young leaves have a surprisingly
nutty flavour and are sometimes
added to early salads or sandwiches.
When fully ripe the vitamin C-rich
fruits are said to have a slight flavour
of avocado pears and are often made
into jellies to add piquancy to cheese
and other savoury dishes.

Hawthorn jelly

Gather the ripe red haws before
birds take them.
• Remove the haws, wash and dry
and ensure the stalks have been
taken off.
• Put the 700 g (1 lb 9 oz) haws in a
heavy saucepan and add 430 ml
(15 fl oz) water.
• Bring to the boil and simmer for
an hour. Mash the berries every 20
minutes with a potato masher.
• Put the mixture in a muslin bag
and allow to drain over night. Do
not squeeze the mixture.
• Place in a clean saucepan and for
every 600 ml (1 pt) of the juice add
450 g (1 lb) of caster (superfine)
sugar. Also add the juice of a lemon.
• Slowly dissolve the sugar and boil
for ten minutes.
• Remove surface foam, and once
the setting point has been reached,
pour into sterilized, warm jars with
screw lids. Store in a cool dark place.

Hop (*Humulus lupulus*)
Also known as: Bine, Common Hop, European Hop

This distinctive perennial herbaceous climber sends up fresh shoots each year that spread 3–4.5 m (10–15 ft) over supports or nearby plants. Twining stems (known as bines) bear deeply cut, three- or five-lobed hairy leaves up to 15 cm (6 in) wide. Pale yellow-green cones (the female parts) are borne in groups of two or three from leaf joints during mid- and late summer, and sometimes slightly later. These cones have been used to brew beer for more than 500 years, providing flavour and stabilizing the brew. The small male flowers are much less distinctive and are normally borne on separate plants.

It is native to southern Europe and into western Asia, but widely distributed as an escapee from cultivation. It was introduced into North America and is widely seen growing wild.

You'll find it: in hedges and thickets, along the edges of farmland or escapees from hop gardens where it was raised abundantly for its part in making beer. It is prevalent in fertile, moisture-retentive soils.

Fruits: these are the hops, which look like inverted cones, about 18 mm (¾ in) long, sometimes more.

Harvesting the fruits: pick the hops individually, taking care not to crush them.

Using the young shoots: young shoots can be cut out in spring, chopped up and boiled as a vegetable. Alternatively, simmer in butter and add to omelettes. A further variation is to cut a handful of young shoots, arrange the cut ends together, tie loosely and immerse in salted water for about an hour. Then wash and plunge into boiling water until tender, usually only a few minutes. Serve drizzled with melted butter or olive oil as a side dish.

Hottentot Fig (*Carpobrotus edulus*)
Also known as: Highway Ice Plant, Sour Fig

You might find this creeping, drought-resis-
tant perennial from South Africa also listed as
Mesembryanthemum edule. Such is its resilience
and adaptability that it has escaped from its
native country and is now established in coastal
areas in many warm, temperate countries.
    Trailing rooting underground stems produce mats
of narrow, upwardly curved thick, triangular-shaped
green moisture-retentive leaves up to 10 cm
(4 in) long. The magenta or yellow flowers are about 5 cm
(2 in) across and appear during early and mid-summer.
In warm countries, flowers often develop earlier and this
brings forward the time when fruits appear.

You'll find it: in sandy ground, banks, loose sand dunes and gravely lime
rich gardens. Its coastal spread is partly due to gulls pulling up stems and
later dropping them, where they develop roots
and produce further colonies.
Fruits: in late summer fleshy, edible,
reddish, fig-shaped fruits, about 36 mm
(1½ in) in diameter and shaped like a
spinning top.
Harvesting the fruits: cut off the fruits
when they become fragrant and colour is
intense. If left, the fruit becomes tough,
leathery and wrinkled.
Using the fruits: can be eaten fresh but
have a strongly sour taste. When able to
ripen in full sun for several weeks the fruits
are used to make a tart-tasting jam.

Ecology warning

In coastal areas in some
countries it has been used to
stabilize sand dunes and gravelly
soil, where it grows rapidly,
stabilizes and assumes command
of large areas, to the detriment
of indigenous plants. Additionally,
where black rats are endemic,
the Hottentot Fig provides
further food for them, with
rats spreading the plant further
through their faeces.

Juniper (*Juniperus communis*)
Also known as: Bastard Killer, Common Juniper, Juniper Berry, Juniper Fruit

This hardy evergreen shrub-like conifer, but sometimes a tree 6 m (20 ft) or more high, has a prickly nature. The needle-like sharply pointed greyish leaves, each with a broad white band on its upper surface, have an apple-like fragrance when crushed.

It is found in wide areas, in northern temperate regions and northwards to the Arctic Circle, where it reveals itself as a dwarf species; also in the mountains of North Africa and the Himalayas, as well as in North America in northern California and Pennsylvania.

You'll find it: an abundant and widespread conifer, native to heaths, moors, pine woods and birch woods, and especially dominant on chalk downs and limestone hills.

Fruits: the round or slightly oval female fruits, about 6 mm (¼ in) across, appear during early summer; in the first year they are green. In the latter part of their second year – usually during late summer and into autumn – they become black and covered with a blue bloom. Each fruit encloses two or three seeds in a resinous, mealy pulp. The small yellow cones are male and are borne on separate plants.

Harvesting the fruits: when gathering ripe berries, wear gloves to protect your hands from the prickly foliage.

Using the fruits: mostly associated with gin, juniper berries have several other culinary uses. Crushed juniper berries, whether fresh or dried, are ideal in marinades for meats, and they are excellent added to pork, goose and beef dishes. Wild game, especially venison, is another great partner to this useful flavouring.

Mother's ruin Gin, which contains juniper as a flavouring, has long had an unflattering association with women and was known in the 18th and 19th centuries as Mother's Ruin. Earlier, berries were eaten to procure abortions (thus the country name Bastard Killer). Nowadays pregnant women, those wishing to become pregnant and nursing mothers should take care not to eat the berries or drink extracts from juniper.

Medlar (*Mespilus germanica*)

A deciduous tree, the Medlar is densely twigged and often with a crooked appearance, thickly clad in thorns and usually under 6 m (20 ft) high. Distinctively, it forms a spreading canopy of dull green crinkled, finely toothed edged lance-like leaves up to 13 cm (5 in) long.

Five-petalled, 5 cm (2 in) wide, saucer-shaped flowers appear at the ends of short, young shoots in the latter part of mid-spring and until early summer, followed by apple-shaped fruits.

Native to Europe and southwest Asia, it is often seen as an escapee from cultivation in other countries. It has been established as a fruit tree in North America and can occasionally be seen as an escapee.

You'll find it: around old and neglected gardens and in orchards in warm areas. Also look for it in ancient hedges and among brambles.
Fruit: round green fruits that resemble very large rose-hips; each has a distinctive five-tailed calyx that partly encapsulates the fruit.
Harvesting the fruits: in warm countries, fruits can be eaten from the tree but in cool climates fruits do not become palatable until half-rotten, sometimes known as 'bletted'. At this stage they become soft and brown. In temperate climates harvest when the weather is dry in late autumn. Place in slatted trays in a frost-proof shed or room until they are ripe (soft and brown) and ready for eating or making into conserves.

Using the fruits: scrape the brown interior flesh from the skin; eat with a dusting of sugar and cream. Medlar jelly is a popular accompaniment for lamb and game. The jelly is also good on scones or toast.

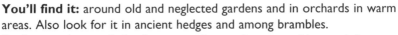

Medlar jelly
Use soft ripened fruits to make jelly.
• Boil medlars in a small amount of water until pulpy, then strain through a jelly bag or muslin cloth.
• Simmer strained juice with sugar (500 g/1 lb 2 oz preserving sugar to each 500 ml/18 fl oz of fruit juice) and a squeeze or two of lemon juice until it reaches setting point.
• Place in sterilized jars once it has cooled, cover and store in a cool dark cupboard.

Mountain Ash (*Sorbus aucuparia*)

Also known as: Common Rowan, European Mountain Ash, Quickbeam, Rowan, Rowan Tree, Wicken-tree

Mountain Ash is a slender and erect deciduous tree that develops a spreading nature with age, usually 6 m (20 ft) high. The 13–23 cm (5–9 in) mid-green leaves are formed of six or seven pairs of narrow leaflets. Clusters of white flowers in flattish heads appear during early and mid-summer. It is native to many temperate parts of Europe and Asia, as well as Morocco. It was taken to North America, where it is now widespread.

Mountain Ash and Crab Apple Jelly

- Remove stalks from the Rowan fruits and wash. Wash the crab apples and cut away bruised and pest-infested parts.
- Place in a heavy-based saucepan, cover with water and simmer until tender.
- Strain the mixture through a muslin bag but do not squeeze. Let all the moisture drain through naturally to avoid clouding the jelly.
- Warm the sugar before putting it into the liquid. For every 500 ml (18 fl oz) of the liquid, measure 500 g (1 lb 2 oz) preserving sugar into an ovenproof dish and place in a moderate oven for 10–15 minutes.
- Put the warmed sugar and strained juice into a saucepan, stir until dissolved, bring to the boil, then simmer until it reaches setting point.
- Skim the surface to remove the scum, and allow to cool slightly.
- While still warm, pour into sterilized jars.

You'll find it: in woods, scrubland and on mountainsides. It is more prevalent in areas with light or slightly acid soil. It can be found as an escapee in fields and hedges.

Fruits: large clusters of round or slightly oval fruits ripen to a rich scarlet or bright red from early to late autumn.

Harvesting the fruits: pick entire clusters of fruits when ripe but before they become soft and mushy.

Using the fruits: the fruits are most commonly used in jelly to accompany game and lamb. They can also be used in combination with Crab Apples to make jelly (see left).

Oregon Grape (*Mahonia aquifolium*)

Also known as: Blue Barberry, Holly Barberry, Holly Grape,
Holly-leaved Barberry, Mountain Grape

A distinctive, hardy, suckering evergreen shrub that grows up to 1.5 m
(5 ft) high and slowly spreads to form sprawling colonies. Its holly-like
leaves are tough, leathery, glossy and dark green, up to 30 cm (12 in) long
and each formed of five to nine leaflets.

During mid- and late spring it develops richly fragrant, golden-yellow
flowers in clustered heads 7.5–13 cm (3–5 in) across. These are followed
in early autumn by masses of berries.

Native to North America from British Columbia to northern California,
it was widely planted in Europe and other countries to provide cover and
food for pheasants. It has spread and become naturalized in many areas.

You'll find it: as an escapee around old and neglected
gardens, alongside fields and on moors, especially where
the soil is moisture-retentive.

Fruits: during early autumn, plants become covered
in clusters of round black berries, slightly more
than 6 mm (¼ in) across and with a violet bloom.
They often appear like miniature grapes and this
has encouraged some of its popular common names,
such as Oregon Grape, Mountain Grape and Holly
Grape.

Harvesting the fruits: pick them in clusters, as
soon as they are ripe and starting to soften.

Using the berries: high in vitamin C, they can be
eaten fresh from the plant although for some
tastes they are tart and best eaten with a dusting
of sugar and cream. Alternatively, the fruits can be
made into a jelly to accompany meat, especially venison
and pork. Berries can be crushed and fermented to produce
a wine, but needs a high proportion of sugar to counteract the
acidity of the brew.

Raspberry (*Rubus idaeus*)

Also known as: European Raspberry, Framboise, Hindberry, Red Raspberry, Wild Raspberry

Raspberry bushes or canes have a suckering, scrambling and sprawling nature, with unbranched stems about 1.5 m (5 ft) long, armoured with slender, straight prickles. The green leaves are formed of several oval, coarsely tooth edged leaflets, 3.6–10 cm (1½–4 in) long.

Clusters of small pinkish flowers appear in clusters at the ends of short twigs that arise on one-year-old stems from early to late summer. Later, these produce the succulent fruits.

It is native to wide areas, from southern Europe to Iceland, into Russia and abundant throughout Asia and much of North America.

You'll find it: in woods and hedgerows, on heaths and especially in hilly areas. It is also a bold escapee and becomes established in hedges, old gardens and allotments. It is spread by birds eating the fruits, so expect to find it over a wide area.

Fruits: ripen to red (only rarely to yellow) from mid-summer to early autumn. Each fruit is formed of several drupelets.

Harvesting fruits: pick as soon fully red and readily part from the stem. Treat carefully as they squash easily, especially when overripe.

Using fruits: they are best eaten fresh but raspberries can be used in hundreds of ways – in cakes, summer puddings, with meringues, fools, and in sauces to accompany ice cream. Chocolate and raspberry is a favourite combination.

Eton Mess

This simple combination of raspberries, broken meringues and whipped cream make the most of foraged summer fruits.

• Pick over a punnet of foraged raspberries to remove leaves, stems and the odd insect.
• Reserving a few raspberries for decoration, add a sprinkling of sugar to the rest of the raspberries and crush with the back of a fork.
• Break up several meringues, then fold whipping cream, crushed berries and meringues together gently.
• Divide into serving dishes and top with a few berries.

Redcurrant (*Ribes rubrum*)

Also known as: Northern Redcurrant, Wineberry

This spreading deciduous shrub, up to 1.5 m (5 ft) high, has three- or five-lobed green leaves, often with heart-shaped bases. Unlike Blackcurrant, which is clump-forming and with many stems arising from ground level, Redcurrant often has just one main stem, with branches growing from it.

During mid- and late spring it develops clusters of saucer-shaped, drooping greenish flowers from leaf joints on the previous season's stems. It is from these flowers that the fruits develop.

Earlier known as *Ribes sativum*, it is native to western Europe and Asia and spreading into Scandinavia and Russia. It is also found in North America and has become naturalized in many other countries.

Redcurrant sauce

To make redcurrant sauce you will need about 450 g (1 lb) redcurrants, 300 g (10 oz) soft brown sugar, two pieces of orange peel, a finely chopped shallot, two sprigs Rosemary and a small wineglass of port.
• Place all the ingredients in a heavy-based saucepan or a preserving pan and heat to a simmer for about 20 minutes, until it becomes sticky and resembles a slightly runny jam.
• Pick out the Rosemary and pieces of orange peel and leave the mixture to cool slightly.
• Before cool, put in clean, sterilized jars and label. Store in a cool dark cupboard and eat with lamb and other roasted meats.

You'll find it: in woods and along hedgerows, where the soil drains well but is moisture-retentive. It also grows in damp rocky places and mountain woods.
Fruits: although it does not fruit as heavily as Blackcurrant, the red, juicy, sweet and shining berries have few rivals in taste and eye-appeal. They ripen during mid-summer.
Harvesting: wait until the fruits are fully ripe, then snip them off in clusters.
Using: like many other types of currant, they are best eaten fresh, with a dusting of sugar. Tarts, jams, jellies and syrups are other options, as well as making redcurrant sauce. Redcurrants are also a mainstay of that perennial favourite, Summer Pudding.

Service Tree *(Sorbus torminalis)*
Also known as: Wild Service Tree, Chequers Tree, Checkers Tree, Chokers Tree

A deciduous tree mostly found in ancient woodlands and hedgerows, it grows to 20 m (65 ft) high and can be 15 m (50 ft) wide, with dark brown to pale grey bark. Its leaves are dark green with three to five pairs of toothed pointed lobes, much like a maple leaf. The white five-petalled flowers are borne in loose, branched clusters in late spring or early summer. It is native to Europe, northwestern Africa and Asia as well as growing in North America as an introduced plant.

You'll find it: in woods, particularly those with oak and ash and in hedgerows. It prefers clay and lime-based soils.
Fruits: shaped like small apples or pears and 12–18 mm (½–¾ in) long, greenish to russet or brown and speckled with rusty lenticels. The fruits are sometimes know as 'chequers'.
Harvesting the fruits: they can be hard, sour and bitter if gathered too soon; wait until mid- to late autumn, but still allow for a period of bletting so that the fruits become almost overripe. Once they reach this stage, they become edible and very sweet.
Using the fruits: Once bletted, the fruits are excellent both raw and cooked. When eaten raw, their taste has been likened to that of plum brandy with overtones of dried apricot. They can also be used in preserves and jellies. In earlier times, before the widespread availability of hops, they were used to flavour beer and to make an alcoholic beverage.

Sloe (*Prunus spinosa*)

Also known as: Blackthorn, Hedge Picks, Wild Plum of Western Europe

A well-known deciduous shrub or small tree, 4–4.5 m (10–15 ft) high, with rigid stems and a much branched nature, it often forms a dense thicket of shoots and spines. Dull green, oval leaves 42 mm (1¾ in) long cluster at the ends of spine-clad stems, with small, pure white flowers appearing singly or in pairs in early or mid-spring on naked stems before the leaves develop.

Originally native across Europe, the Mediterranean regions to Persia, and Asia, it has been introduced in many places, including North America, and is established as an escapee.

You'll find it: in hedgerows, open woods and scrubland, often growing in poor soil, although it does demand plenty of sunshine.

Fruits: are round and about 12 mm (½ in) across, blue at first but when ripe a beautiful shiny black, and often have a slight bloom.

Harvesting the fruits: pick when ripe, in mid-autumn; pull off, complete with their small stalks. At this stage they are tart and acidic. Place in trays and put in a cool place indoors.

Using the fruits: the fruit's main claim to fame is in delicious Sloe gin, for which there are many recipes.

Sloe gin

- Use a large, wide-necked (but sealable) sterilized jar or bottle.
- Wash the ripe sloes, dry and prick with a sharp knife or fork.
- Half fill the jar or bottle with fruits. Then add sugar (about one-quarter of the weight of the sloes is about right), and top up with gin.
- Add a drop or two of almond essence and a small cinnamon stick.
- Seal the jar then shake to mix the sugar and gin with the sloes; place in a cool, dark cupboard. Repeat the mixing daily for two or three weeks. Then allow to stand undisturbed for three or four months.
- Pour off the juice, which by now is a deep, ruby red and can be drunk in modest amounts. Place the sloe gin in a screw-capped bottle.
- The fruits will be soft, edible and steeped in gin, so take care! Try a few with ice cream.

Whitebeam (*Sorbus aria*)

Also known as: Chess Apple, Hen Apple, Whitten, Whittenbeam

This deciduous tree, occasionally a shrub, is usually 7.5–9 m (25–30 ft) high, sometimes more. It forms a dense crown of branches that become smothered with oval, occasionally pear-shaped, green leaves up to 10 cm (4 in) long and coated on their undersides in a dense, white felt.

During late spring and early summer it develops 5–7.5 cm (2–3 in) wide clustered heads of dull-white flowers, each about 12 mm (½ in) wide.

It is native throughout central and southern Europe, including southern Spain, Italy and Corsica. It has been planted as a decorative tree in many countries, including North America.

You'll find it: in woods and scrubland on chalk and in limestone soils. It is spread by birds eating the fruits, so look for it on the fringes of woods as well as in more open sites, and especially in suburbs of towns where it has been planted as a street tree.

Fruits: the oval or round fruits, about 12 mm (½ in) long, appear in late summer and ripen to scarlet red in autumn.

Harvesting the fruits: cut them from the tree in bunched clusters when most of the fruits are richly ripe; place in trays in a cool room.

Using the fruits: like several other fruits, when newly harvested they are inedible and best left until bletted. To do this, store in trays in a cool, dry place until they are almost going rotten. It is only at this stage that they are edible and have acquired the flavour of luscious tropical fruits. They can be made into a jelly on their own, or mixed with rosehips. Additionally, when harvested fruits can be slowly dried in a slightly warm oven, then ground into a powder and mixed with a cereal such as wheat.

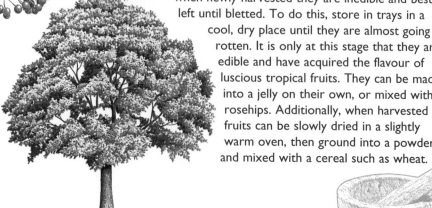

Wild Cherry (*Prunus avium*)

Also known as: Bird Cherry, Brandy Mazzard, Crab
Cherry, Gean, Massard, Mazzard, Sweet Cherry

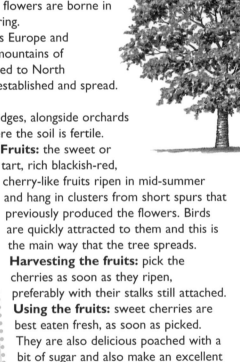

A lofty deciduous tree, the Wild Cherry grows up
to 18 m (60 ft) high, open-branched with shiny,
smooth, reddish-brown peeling bark. The oval,
light dull-green leaves usually have a drawn-out
point and are 7.5–13 cm (3–5 in) long. Pure white,
five-petalled, slightly cup-shaped flowers are borne in
clusters during mid- and late spring.

   Native and widespread across Europe and
western Asia, as well as in the mountains of
northern Africa, it was introduced to North
America, where it has become established and spread.

You'll find it: in woods and hedges, alongside orchards
and farmland and especially where the soil is fertile.

Fruits: the sweet or
tart, rich blackish-red,
cherry-like fruits ripen in mid-summer
and hang in clusters from short spurs that
previously produced the flowers. Birds
are quickly attracted to them and this is
the main way that the tree spreads.

Harvesting the fruits: pick the
cherries as soon as they ripen,
preferably with their stalks still attached.

Using the fruits: sweet cherries are
best eaten fresh, as soon as picked.
They are also delicious poached with a
bit of sugar and also make an excellent
pie filling or cobbler. Those with a
bitter taste are better used to create
cherry brandy.

Cherry brandy

There are many recipes for making
cherry brandy. This one is simple.
• Remove stalks from the cherries,
then wash and allow them to dry.
Prick each cherry several times to
encourage the absorption of brandy.
• Fill a clean, wide-necked sterilized
bottle that can be sealed with a lid to
three-quarters full with cherries.
• Add a couple of tablespoons of
sugar, depending on the sweetness
of the cherries.
• Fill the bottle to the top with
cheap brandy, seal the bottle or jar
and shake thoroughly.
• Leave in a cool, dark cupboard
until Christmas, where a tasty and
alcoholic treat awaits you.

Wild Rose (*Rosa canina*)

Also known as: Briar Rose, Brier Rose, Dog Berries, Dog Briar, Dog Brier, Dog Rose, Wild Dog Rose

With its long arching stems, up to 3 m (10 ft) long and packed with curved or hooked prickles, the Wild Rose provides a formidable fortress for the flowers and fruits. The dull green leaves are formed of 5–7 broadly oval leaflets, each up to 36 mm (1½ in) long. During early and mid-summer, white or pinkish sweetly scented, five-petalled flowers are borne singly or in small clusters along the stems.

Widespread and common throughout Europe it has been introduce to many other countries, including North America and the Antipodes. The Wild Rose has been used as rootstock for varieties of cultivated roses and from that role has spread and become naturalized in many areas.

You'll find it: in hedges, scrubland and woods, where it usually entangles itself with other plants and produces a wide clump of prickly stems.

Fruits: known as rosehips and occasionally Pixie Ears, Dog Berries and Dog Hips, the round or egg-shaped fruits ripen to a rich bright red.

Harvesting the fruits and flowers: gather the petals when one or two have dropped from the flowers and use soon after. Fruits, which are a good source of vitamin C, are gathered when richly coloured in autumn, preferrably after the first frost.

Using the fruits and flowers: petals can be used in salads, jams, rose-petal jelly, Turkish delight and rose vinegar, while the fruits are famed in preserves, syrups and jellies. They are rich in vitamin C and, during times of hardship and scarcity of other fruits, have been made into rosehip syrup that was given to children to keep colds at bay.

Wild Strawberry (*Fragaria vesca*)

**Also known as: Sow-teat's Strawberry,
Woodland Strawberry**

A perennial plant with a thick, woody base producing long runners that develop roots at their leaf joints, its leaves are usually formed of three oval and coarsely serrated leaflets, bright green above and pale green beneath. White five-petalled flowers with deep yellow centres, up to 18 mm (¾ in) across, appear on short stalks from mid-spring to mid-summer.

It is native to southern Europe, North America, Madeira and Azores and much of Asia. It has also been planted in warm and temperate regions, from where it has escaped into the countryside.

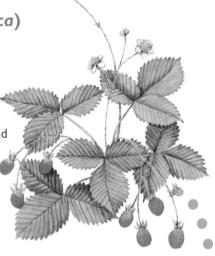

Cava and Wild Strawberry Jellies

Make the most of a handful of delicious wild berries in this summery jelly.
• Soak 4 gelatine leaves in cold water for 5 minutes. Squeeze out excess water.
• In a small bowl over a pan of water, measure 100 ml (4 oz) of the Cava, add the gelatine and 1 tablespoon sugar and heat through.
• Remove from the heat and add 250 ml (8 oz) cold Cava and stir.
• Place a few berries in the base of four wine glasses or other pretty dessert dishes.
• Pour over the gelatine and Cava mixture, then refrigerate until set.
• Garnish with a few more berries if you have any left.

You'll find it: in woods, grassland and scrubland, especially where the soil is fertile and slightly chalky.

Fruits: small, intensely flavoured fruits, about 12 mm (½ in) across and usually red, they have a sublime flavour compared with commercial berries.

Harvesting the fruits: pick as soon as they are red, usually in late summer. If left on the plant too long they quickly deteriorate.

Using the fruits: best eaten fresh, either on their own or with cream. They are usually sweet enough not to require a dusting of sugar.

Wild nuts

Botanical definitions of nuts can be confusing, so here it is used in its popular sense for any seed or fruit enclosed in a hard or brittle shell. Trees are our main source of nuts, which are mainly harvested in autumn and range from acorns to walnuts. Rich in protein, fats and oils, nuts are a nutritious and healthy addition to a modern diet and certainly provided our forebears with valuable calories. For example, 450 g (1 lb) of walnuts provides about 3,000 calories, while Beech mast (nuts of the Beech tree) yields up to 20 per cent of its volume in an oil rich in minerals, vitamins and proteins.

Nuts quickly provide foragers with large amounts of nutritious food, but these nuts are often an essential part of stored food for wild animals, enabling them to survive throughout winter; therefore, do not strip trees bare of nuts.

After harvesting nuts, keep dry as they decay quickly if damp and placed in a cupboard with little air circulation. When nuts are collected while still damp – perhaps after a few weeks of continuous rain – they need to be dried in slight warmth in a well-ventilated place before being stored for use in late autumn or winter.

For many early peoples throughout the world, long before wheat and barley were domesticated, nuts such as acorns were a major source of food. Apart from feeding early men and women, acorns were a central food for the animals they hunted, including deer, wild turkeys, squirrels and wild fowl. In many areas the challenge to eat and survive was met by acorns – a simple and unprepossessing nut.

This chapter describes five sources of nuts for foragers in temperate climates, but there are many others in warm climates, including Australian native plants such as Queensland Nuts and Moreton Bay Chestnut. Brazil Nuts are native to South America, while Cashew Nuts are at home in tropical America. In Mediterranean regions, Pine Kernels are eaten like peanuts, either raw or roasted.

Beech (*Fagus sylvatica*)

Also known as: Common Beech, European Beech

This stately deciduous tree has few equals, often standing 30 m (100 ft) high and forming a canopy of vein-lined, oval and pointed, shiny-green leaves. In early autumn, the tree produces a mass of nuts that for centuries have been eaten as food as well as providing forage for pigs, deer and other animals. Native to wide areas of western and central Europe, including Corsica, Sicily and Greece, it has been planted in many temperate regions in both hemispheres, from where it has spread into the wild.

You'll find it: in well-drained, open woodland, parks and grassland, especially where the soil is chalky.

Nuts: known as beech mast, each nut is triangular, 15 mm (⅝ in) long and borne in pairs. They are enclosed in a hard, woody, pear-shaped, four-lobed husk and covered in bristles. Beech trees bear nuts only once every three or four years, but when this happens their harvest is prodigious.

Harvesting beech mast (nuts): these ripen and fall in early to mid-autumn. Collect as soon as possible, before they are taken by squirrels, deer, badgers and dormice, then place in slatted boxes in a ventilated, gently warm room. Some may need to dry slightly if previously dampened by rain.

Using beech mast: highly nutritious, the nuts are eaten raw or roasted and salted. Additionally, freshly harvested nuts yield up to 20 per cent of their volume in an oil rich in minerals, vitamins and proteins. Extracting the oil to use as a butter substitute as well as in general cooking involves cleaning the beech mast, removing the husks and placing in a liquidizer or fine mincing machine. Put the pulp-like material in a muslin bag and press to express the oil, then pour resulting oil into dry, sterilized, well-sealed jars. It needs to be used within a few months.

Hazel (*Corylus avellana*)

Also known as: Cob, Cobnut, European Filbert, European Hazelnut, Filbeard, Filbert, Nutall

The deciduous, shrub-like Hazel grows up to
6 m (20 ft) high and you will notice its pendulous,
bright-yellow, male catkins in mid- and late winter,
long before its clusters of nuts are ready to be
harvested in autumn. The female catkins are less
apparent, being short and bud-like. Broadly oval,
tooth-edged green leaves appear in spring and
assume rich yellow shades in autumn.
   Native to Europe, it has been planted in
many temperate climates, including parts of
North America.

You'll find it: growing in hedgerows and at shoulder-
height or less, a result of being regularly cut back; also
in woods and on scrubland.
Nuts: round to oval, each nut is 12–18 mm (½–¾ in)
long and borne in clusters of up to four in autumn. Each has a hard brown
shell partially enclosed in a thick, deeply lobed green husk.
Harvesting the nuts: they remain on the tree until ripe and fall off in
the latter part of early autumn. At this stage, the husks (the protective
outer parts) will have changed from green to brown. The nuts inside
should be firm; if gathered too early they will be soft and tasteless and not
store well. Remove the husks and store the nuts, still in their shells, in a
warm, dry place, but do not allow them to dry out fully. When ripe, the
shell naturally falls away from the nut.
Using nuts: highly nutritious and eaten raw, the nuts are chopped for
adding to salads, or used as a substitute for almonds. The ground nuts
can be blended with milk or yoghurt to make a nutritious smoothie using
one part nuts to three of milk (add honey to taste). Hazel nuts are also
delicious roasted, and are good added to cereals, breads and cakes. The
pressed nuts also yield a very good oil for salads and cooking.

Common Oak (*Quercus robur*)
Also known as: English Oak, Pedunculate Oak, Truffle Oak

This lofty, often 25 m (80 ft) high deciduous tree is better known for its timber than its ability to provide food. However, nearly 2000 years ago the Roman writer Pliny the Younger (61–112 AD) wrote of 13 varieties of oak tree with acorns that could be ground to produce a bread-making flour, and nearly 1000 years ago, the English Domesday Book described acorns being fed to hogs.

Native throughout Europe, western Asia and North Africa, it has been planted in many regions of the world with temperate climates, including parts of North America.

You'll find it: in forests, but not where other trees tightly encroach upon it. You will also see it in open countryside and alongside hedgerows and paths. It grows best in warm temperate regions, as late spring frosts damage early developing shoots.

Acorn coffee

In times of privation, coffee-drinkers have turned to acorns as a coffee substitute. Many other plants, including dandelions, chicory and grains of corn and rye, are also used to produce a coffee-type drink. Several ways are recommended to create nutty tasting acorn coffee, including:
- Gather fallen acorns, remove their cupped bases and place in boiling water until soft. Allow to cool slightly then remove the shells.
- Cut them in half or quarters and put on low in a microwave until dry.
- Then place on a baking tray (cookie sheet) in a warm oven and roast until brown.
- Once cool place in a coffee grinder or kitchen blender and grind to the consistency of coffee grains.
- Use grounds to make drip coffee or espresso as you would with regular coffee grounds.

Acorns: a small rounded nut (botanically a fruit), the humble acorn is well known. Each acorn usually takes a couple of seasons to mature and is formed of a cup that holds the nut. Trees do not usually produce acorns until 20 years old and may not crop until about 40 years old.

Harvesting the nuts: trees shed their acorns (when ripe) in early autumn, usually slightly earlier than the fall of leaves. Some acorns will be green, most brown.

Using the nuts: for thousands of years preparing flour from acorns has been traditional among native people of many lands; in times of famine it became an essential food for many people. Today, it is regaining popularity, especially among back-to-nature enthusiasts. In North America, indigenous peoples are said to have mixed clay with acorn flour (at a ratio, by weight, of one of washed clay to twenty of flour). The resulting bread is claimed to be sweet and to rise as if yeast had been added.

Acorn flour

- Gather fallen acorns, green or brown, immediately as they are available; do not let them remain on the grass to become dirty and wet.
- Place in a clean bucket; expect each container to produce half that amount of flour.
- Arrange the acorns on a baking tray (cookie sheet) and roast for 20–30 minutes in an oven at 120°C (250°F). This will both dry them and kill any insects lurking inside. When cool, crack off the now-brittle shells to release the acorns.
- Place the acorns in a muslin bag and immerse in water for two weeks, changing it two or three times each day. This removes most of the tannins, which if left impart a bitter taste to the flour.
- Either sun-dry on a windowsill or place in a just warm oven until totally free from moisture. Store the acorns in clean, moisture-proof jars or immediately grind to a flour. If stored, use as soon as possible.
- The flour can be used in place of wheat; it is ideal for making pancakes, muffins and, of course, acorn bread.

Sweet Chestnut (*Castanea sativa*)

Also known as: Eurasian Chestnut, European Chestnut, Spanish Chestnut

A large deciduous tree, up to 30 m (100 ft) high, the Sweet Chestnut produces nuts in mid- to late autumn that can be eaten raw or roasted. Its distinctive, shiny, deep green and narrowly oval leaves are edged in soft spines. Yellow, erect or spreading male catkins, up to 15 cm (6 in) long, appear in mid-summer, while the green female flowers (borne at the bases of male catkins) are sparse but by autumn will have developed into nuts.

Native to Europe, North Africa, southern Turkey and western Iran, it has been planted and established in many temperate climates. It is well-known in North America.

You'll find it: usually in woods surrounded by other trees, or in parks and open countryside. Sometimes it is coppiced every 10–15 years (cut down to near ground level in late winter) to produce young, straight stems used for fencing.

Nuts: triangular, bright red-brown nuts, borne in twos or threes and each 18–30 mm (¾–1¼ in) across, are enclosed in pale green husks. These husks, often known as burs, are covered with prickles.

Harvesting the nuts: trees start to shed their nuts in mid-autumn; you will not be able to reach most them but they can be knocked off by using a stick. They can be eaten raw if the husk (which is prickly) and bitter inner skin are removed. But they are more often roasted; slit the husks and either put them on a grate close to a fire, or in hot ash. As a guide to when they are ready, put an uncut one next to them and when its outer parts burst (usually with a bang) the others are ready to eat.

Using the nuts: apart from eating the nuts raw or roasted, they can be ground or chopped and used in soup, as stuffing for turkey, in jams and cakes. Small nuts can be ground into a flour for making bread or pancakes. The nuts roasted, then ground. The yellowish, slightly fragrant flour is ideal in cakes and breads but is usually reluctant to rise, therefore, add an equal amount of wheat flour.

Walnut (*Juglans regia*)

Also known as: English Walnut,
Persian Walnut, Madeira Nut

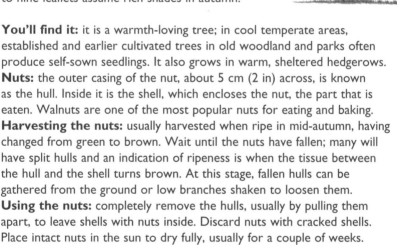

Native to China, west and central Asia and
southeastern Europe, this large, deciduous
tree, up to 30 m (100 ft) high, is now widely
naturalized in Europe. It has also been planted in
other countries, where it has spread. However, in
North America the native Black Walnut (*Juglans
nigra*) is more popular and widespread.

The large, distinctive, shiny green leaves of seven
to nine leaflets assume rich shades in autumn.

You'll find it: it is a warmth-loving tree; in cool temperate areas,
established and earlier cultivated trees in old woodland and parks often
produce self-sown seedlings. It also grows in warm, sheltered hedgerows.
Nuts: the outer casing of the nut, about 5 cm (2 in) across, is known
as the hull. Inside it is the shell, which encloses the nut, the part that is
eaten. Walnuts are one of the most popular nuts for eating and baking.
Harvesting the nuts: usually harvested when ripe in mid-autumn, having
changed from green to brown. Wait until the nuts have fallen; many will
have split hulls and an indication of ripeness is when the tissue between
the hull and the shell turns brown. At this stage, fallen hulls can be
gathered from the ground or low branches shaken to loosen them.
Using the nuts: completely remove the hulls, usually by pulling them
apart, to leave shells with nuts inside. Discard nuts with cracked shells.
Place intact nuts in the sun to dry fully, usually for a couple of weeks.
They can then be stored in a cool, dry place for several months.

They are often used as late autumn and winter 'treats', chopped in
cakes and biscuits. Walnuts are delicious with pears and any blue cheese
in a winter salad. Shelled nuts can be kept in the refrigerator for up
to five months, and in the freezer for more than a year.

In addition to ripe walnuts, you can use young, green fruits,
gathered before the nut-case hardens; these are
sometimes pickled in vinegar for later use.

Mushrooms, truffles and other edible fungi

Foraging, picking and eating checks

Even if you are confident in your ability to identify fungi, there are still a few things to keep in mind:

- Ensure you have legal rights to take the fungi; do not traipse over private land or destroy growing crops.
- Do not forage for fungi on a wet day as many are highly porous, which spoils their texture and taste.
- Before picking fungi, check that it complies with its description and picture. Remember that colour, size and shape may vary during its growth.
- Do not pull fungi directly out of the ground. Instead, carefully twist its stem until it comes away from the soil.
- Before placing fungi in a well-ventilated basket, use a sharp knife to cut off the stem's base.
- Check for maggots or insects in the cap area; if present in large numbers, throw the fungi away. Also discard fungi that are decaying or reveal white gills (many poisonous types have this characteristic).
- Before eating, either raw or cooked, brush off dirt. If it is necessary to wash fungi, immediately dry the surface with a paper towel.
- When you get your fungi home, recheck their authenticity. Then, place in a well-ventilated room and use within 24 hours.

Throughout the centuries, mushrooms have gained a dark and sinister reputation. Certainly some fungi are deadly poisonous when eaten, while many others are a valuable source of food and are highly prized by chefs and foragers throughout the world. Identifying fungi that can be eaten is not easy, as apart from their limited growing and harvesting period each year (when you can get to know and identify them), many often change shape and colour throughout their lives.

It is vitally important that you correctly identify any fungi you collect and plan to eat. The best way to gain knowledge is by learning from someone who knows fungi well – some experts offer courses and lead guided forays in the autumn. And although most mushrooms are relatively easy to identify, there are a number of poisonous look-alikes and about 20 species that are very, very dangerous indeed!

Unless you are very familiar with a species, do not rely on the photographs or illustrations in a book for identification, especially since many change their appearance throughout their life cycle. If you are not sure about the identification of a particular specimen you wish to eat and cannot with certainty identify it, discard it. Place it in a plastic bag (so that children and family pets cannot sample it) and put in a rubbish bin.

If, by chance, you become unwell after eating a fungi, contact a doctor immediately and where possible take along a sample of the particular fungi. Additionally, write down the name of the species you think you have eaten, as this may lead to rapid identification of the 'lookalike' fungi you have mistakenly consumed. And remember that although symptoms from some poisonous fungi may arise within minutes, others take several days to emerge.

BLEWITS:

Wood Blewit (*Lepista nuda*)
Also known as: Pied Bleu

A largish mushroom with a lilac to purple-pink cap 6–13 cm (2½–5 in) across, convex or shield-shaped; with age it assumes reddish shades. The entire mushroom has a sweet and perfume-like scent, with thick, lilac-blue flesh. It is native to North America and Europe and also introduced into Australia.

You'll find it: in coniferous and deciduous woodland, as well as gardens.
Harvesting the fungi: from autumn to early winter.
Eating the fungi: best cooked rather than eaten fresh. Eat soon after gathering, as they are often infested with fly larvae and do not store well.

Field Blewit (*Lepista saeva*)
Also known as: Blue Leg, Pied Violet

Less common than the Wood Blewit, it has a smooth, slightly domed cap up to 12 cm (4½ in) across and 6 cm (2½ in) high; old ones have flatter caps and sometimes develop wavy edges. The cap is greyish or brown, tinged lilac or purple, while the stem is whitish with blue streaks and slightly bulbous at its base. The whole fungi has a strong, sweet, perfume-like scent, with white to greyish-pink flesh. Widely found in Europe and North America.

You'll find it: on grassland and occasionally in lightly shaded woods; it mostly grows in chalky conditions.
Harvesting the fungi: late summer to very late autumn.
Eating the fungi: they can be eaten fresh (but sometimes cause indigestion) so are usually cooked. Eat soon after gathering, as they are often infested with fly larvae and do not store well. Excellent when sautéd in butter or as an addition to omelettes.

Cep (*Boletus edulus*)

Also known as: King Bolete, Penny Bun, Penny Bun Boletus, Porcini

This large wild mushroom is one of the safest to gather as there are no poisonous species that closely resemble it. On maturity, its cap is 7.5–25 cm (3–10 in) across, slightly sticky to touch, convex when young but flattening with age. The cap is usually reddish-brown, fading to white near the edges, with the whole top darkening as it matures. The stem is stout and swollen, pale brown and revealing a network of raised, white veins towards its top.

The flesh, which has a mild nutty flavour, is firm and white when young, becoming spongy with age.

Ceps occur throughout northern temperate regions of North America, Europe and Asia. Additionally, it has been introduced to southern Africa and New Zealand.

You'll find it: in coniferous and deciduous woodland and especially in grassy clearings. It is common in Beech woods.

Harvesting the fungi: late summer to mid-autumn and sometimes slightly later.

Eating the fungi: it is low in fat and digestible carbohydrates, but high in vitamins, proteins and minerals. Ceps are superb when sliced and eaten fresh, although widely eaten sautéd. They are frequently dried and used in casseroles, soups and risottos. It is also good in pasta dishes as well as lending itself to to being stuffed with chopped onions, bacon and parsley, and bread crumbs, then baked until tender.

Other edible Boletus

• Bay Boletus (*Boletus badius*): chestnut-brown cap, 5–13 cm (2–5 in) wide, with fairly soft, white or lemon yellow flesh. It is ready for harvesting from late summer to mid- or even late autumn. It occurs in both coniferous and deciduous woodland, especially under Beech trees.

• Yellow-cracked Boletus (*Boletus subtomentosus*): olive yellow to rich yellow cap, 5–12 cm (2–4½ in) wide, becoming reddish-brown with age. The flesh is white or pale lemon yellow. Usually ready for harvesting from late summer and into early autumn. Again it is often seen in deciduous woodland.

Chanterelle (*Cantharellus cibarius*)
Also known as: Chanterelle Commune, Girolles, Golden Chanterelle

The funnel-shaped cap is egg yellow to orange yellow, sometimes paler, with flesh that has an apricot scent but when eaten produces a fruity and mildly peppery taste. It is up to 10 cm (4 in) wide, sometimes slightly more, initially round and flat but later with a depressed centre and assuming its distinctive funnel shape with irregularly waved edges. However, there are a number of other mushrooms that looks similar (see warning box below), so make sure that you are absolutely correct in your identification.

It is native to northern and temperate parts of Europe and North America, including Mexico, and is also found in Asia and parts of Africa.

You'll find it: in woodland, especially under oaks, birches, beech and pine trees, and where the soil is slightly acid.

Harvesting the fungi: gather from mid-summer through to early autumn, depending on the rain fall and temperature.

Eating the fungi: after cutting, trim the base and use a soft brush to clean the flesh. Chanterelles are inevitably used fresh since they do not dry well. There are many ways to eat them, including sautéd in butter with parsley and used as a side dish. Chanterelles are also delicious when added to scrambled eggs, omelettes and pasta dishes. Pan-roasted Chanterelles make a great accompaniment to lemon sole and oysters.

Beware

There are several 'lookalike' species that must be avoided, including:
- False Chanterelle (*Hygrophoropsis aurantiaca*), which is inedible
- Jack O'Lantern (*Omphalotus olearius*) also known as Copper Trumpet, which is extremely poisonous
- Deadly Webcap (*Cortinarius rubellus*), which is deadly poisonous and causes kidney failure. It was earlier known as *Cortinarius speciosissimus*

Fairy-ring Champignon (*Marasmius oreades*)
Also known as: Fairy Ring Mushroom, Scotch Bonnet

This mushroom species grows in fairy-rings on lawns; this one – as well as a few others – is edible, but others are not, so take great care with identification (see warning box below).

It develops brownish caps, often tinged pink to pale reddish-brown, up to 5 cm (2 in) across, initially domed then flattened and with even, uplifted edges. This mushroom has a creamy, woody (often claimed to resemble saw-dust), mushroom-like scent.

This mushroom is native and widespread in Europe and North America.

You'll find it: in lawns, pastures and fields with short grass, as well as along roadsides. It forms circles of fungi, disfiguring lawns and golf courses.
Harvesting the fungi: late spring to late autumn, but most abundant in summer.
Eating the fungi: the white to buff flesh tends to be thin and rather tough, but with a pleasant, mushroom-like flavour. Caps have the tendency to dry quickly, when they become hard and leathery and change to a pale tan colour. Stems are usually discarded if they become dry.

Traditionally, the caps have been threaded on to strings (with a button on the bottom) and hung up to dry, where they can remain in a warm but well-ventilated room for several weeks. They can be reconstituted by soaking in clean water for several hours. Alternatively, instead of rehydrating in water, simply drop them as they are into soups and stews.

> **Beware**
> There are several 'lookalike' species that occur in similar situations and close to Fairy-ring Champignon that must be avoided, including:
> • Ivory Clitocybe (*Clitocybe dealbata*), which is deadly poisonous
> • False Champignon (*Clitocybe rivulosa*), which is also deadly poisonous

Field Mushroom (*Agaricus campestris*)

Also known as: Champignons, Common Field Mushroom, Common Mushroom, Hot-bed Mushroom, Meadow Mushroom, Pink Bottoms, Rosé des prés

An attractive mushroom with creamy white caps, about 3–10 cm (1¾–4 in) wide, on stems 2–6 cm (⅞–2½ in) long. Initially, caps are dome-shaped, later flattening slightly and, with age, assume a brownish tinge. The white flesh is slightly reddish-pink to brown when cut. It is closely related to the cultivated Button Mushroom (*Agaricus bisporus*), which is widely sold in shops and supermarkets. The Field Mushroom occurs in many temperate areas of Europe, as well as in North America, Australia, Asia, southern Africa and Afghanistan.

You'll find it: in large fairy-rings on lawns, in meadows and fields, especially where manured by livestock.

Harvesting the fungi: from mid-summer to late autumn; especially abundant where the climate is mild and after showers of rain.

Eating the fungi: at their best when sliced and fresh in salads, although some claim that the flavour intensifies when cooked, especially with large and mature specimens. Its uses are endless – try in soups and risottos, make mushroom paté, or sauté in butter and serve on toast covered with their own juices.

Beware

There are several 'lookalike' species that must be avoided:
• Destroying Angel (*Amanita virosa*): take care when picking Field Mushrooms at the button stage as it then resembles this infamous mushroom. This fatal fungus has the sickly sweet scent of honey and a pure white cap that is frequently slightly sticky to the touch
• Death Cap (*Amanita phalloides*) is another deadly fungi sometimes confused with the Field Mushroom
• Deadly Fibrecap (*Inocybe patouill-dii*) occurs in similar locations as Field Mushroom but is deadly poisonous

Giant Puff-ball (*Calvatia gigantea*)

Sometimes known as *Langermannia gigantea*, this is a monster of the fungus world; giant specimens are said to have been mistaken for sheep! Usually it is 20–50 cm (8–20 in) across. The flesh is white and firm when young and this is when it should be eaten; later it becomes yellowish, then brown (when it is best left alone). Its matt surface is white at first and finely textured like kid gloves. Later, the surface discolours to pale olive-brown.

It is widely seen in temperate regions throughout the northern and southern hemispheres. In some countries in Europe, such as parts of Poland, it is now protected, while in others, including Lithuania and Norway, it is considered rare. In many other countries there is concern about its decreasing numbers, therefore, do not over-forage this fungi.

You'll find it: in fields, gardens and deciduous forests, along hedgerows and edges of fields, and on banks. It is sometimes found growing among stinging nettles, which offers it some protection from animals and foragers.
Harvesting the fungi: in late summer into autumn.
Eating the fungi: it should be eaten while young, when the flesh is firm and white. Try it thinly sliced and and added in salads. Alternatively, thicker slices can be coated in beaten egg and breadcrumbs, then sautéd like cutlets – serve with a squeeze of lemon. You can also add it cubed to stews and casseroles, where it takes on a delicious meaty texture.

Another edible puffball The Mosaic Puffball (*Calvatia utriformis*) has a white to cream, pear-shaped body that can reach 25 cm (10 in) across and 20 cm (8 in) high, with white flesh that, with age, becomes greenish-yellow, later dark olive-brown. Its outer surface cracks into hexagonal patches as it ages, hence its common name.

It is widespread in northern temperate regions and found on pastures and sandy heaths during late summer and into autumn; the flesh is edible when young.

Morel (*Morchella esculenta*)

Also known as: Common Morel, Dryland Fish, Haystack, May Mushroom, Morel Mushroom, Molly Moocher, Morille Comestible, Sponge Morel, True Morel, Yellow Morel

This distinctive fungus, growing 10–20 cm (4–6 in) high, has a cap that begins life as a tightly compressed greyish sponge, with lighter coloured ridges. It then expands to create a large, yellowish, honeycomb-like sponge with ridges and deep pits. The stout, sometimes twisted white stem becomes yellowish and reddish with age while the cap is hollow. It is native to North America, as well as throughout much of Europe.

You'll find it: usually in woodland clearings, especially in chalky soil around deciduous trees, old orchards, bases of well established hedgerows and where vegetation has been cleared through burning. It grows singly or in groups.

Harvesting the fungi: mid- to late spring – it has a narrow time band when it can be gathered each year. However, in northern parts of North America, gathering is usually delayed until early summer, when the temperature rises and the weather improves. This delay also applies to colder regions in Europe.

Eating the fungi: Morels should **not** be eaten raw as they contain small amounts of toxins that are removed through cooking. Because of their honeycomb-like hollow structure, morels become a refuge for insects. Cut lengthways and wash in running water (take care to dry in a warm room) or dust with a small, soft artist's brush. Morels are popular in soups and stews, and are excellent stuffed. They can also be sautéd in butter.

> **Beware**
> There are 'lookalike' species that must be avoided, including:
> • False Morel or Turban Fungus (*Gyromitra esculenta*), which may be fatal when eaten raw and very harmful to some even when cooked

Oyster Mushroom (*Pleurotus ostreatus*)
Also known as: Flat Mushroom, Oyster Cap, Oyster Fungus

Sometimes considered to be flavourless, this bracket fungus was widely collected during times of food scarcity, especially as it is easy to gather, grows in colonies, and dries and keeps well. The caps, 5–15 cm (2–6 in) across but occasionally slightly larger, do not usually have stems and grow directly from their host. The caps are deep bluish-grey to grey-brown, depending on their age; the narrow, crowded gills are white to greyish. The entire fungus has a pleasant, almond-like scent. It is widespread throughout the world, in temperate as well as subtropical forests.

You'll find it: because it is a primary decomposer of dead and dying trunks and branches, you will find it among deciduous trees especially Beech and Ash. It is only occasionally found on conifers. However, it does not like growing near stinging nettles, which like an acidic soil.
Harvesting the fungi: throughout the year, especially in warm and moist areas. In temperate regions, they are mainly gathered in autumn and winter. It should be harvested while young, since the flesh becomes tough and the flavour unpleasant with age.
Eating the fungi: it is considered a delicacy in oriental cuisine and frequently served on its own or in soups, stews, casseroles, stuffed or in stir-fry recipes. Try it lightly grilled. It can also be dried successfully and stores well in jars under good olive oil or wine vinegar.

Shaggy Parasol (*Chlorophyllum rhacodes*)

Formerly known as *Lepiota rhacodes* and *Macrolepiota rhacodes*, this mushroom has a distinctive cap that is 7.5–18 cm (3–7 in) across when mature. When young, however, it is smaller and resembles a drumstick. It can be both dull- or dirty-brown and has a rough, scaly and shaggy appearance (hence the name). On maturity the cap flattens. The soft white flesh becomes reddish-brown if cut or bruised, with a strong, pleasant smell. The stem, up to 15 cm (6 in) high, is whitish and bulbous-based. Note that there are a number of poisonous species that resemble this fungi, so be especially careful about identification (see below).

The form *hortensis* is sometimes found in manure-rich gardens and large old greenhouses. It is more robust and larger than the species and reveals an almost white, coarse, scaly cap, brown at its centre, with an extremely bulbous stem.

The species is native to Europe and North America, although with disagreements and re-classification over the years, some think that it is also found in Australia.

You'll find it: in woodland and especially where there is a deep litter of leaves or needles from conifers. It flourishes in rich soil in light shade.

Harvesting the fungi: mid-summer through to late autumn.

Eating the fungi: although it is a good edible mushroom, some people react unfavourably to it, so take care when eating for the first time. To be on the safe side it should always be cooked. Also discard the stems of all but the very youngest of specimens. It can be added to soups, casseroles and stews, as well as being sautéd. It also makes a welcome accompaniment to bacon in a bacon and mushroom quiche. This fungi can be dried and then reconstituted.

Beware

There are 'lookalike' species that must be avoided, including:
• False Parasol or Green-spored Parasol (*Chlorophyllum molybdites*): is a widespread, highly poisonous look-alike species (it is apparently the most commonly consumed poisonous mushroom in North America). It also grows in similar habitat to the edible Shaggy Parasol and Parasol mushrooms

Truffle (*Tuber aestivum*)
Also known as: Summer Truffle

The truffle is perhaps one of the best-known and highly prized edible fungi, widely sought by chefs and very expensive to buy. It grows and develops underground in association with Beech, Sweet Chestnut and evergreen oak trees, and is usually seen when 5–15 cm (2–6 in) across. Irregularly round, dark brown, lumpy and warty, it has firm white flesh that turns buff with a network of white veins.

It is native to wide areas throughout Europe, from east to west and into southern regions, where it is highly prized and often strictly protected.

You'll find it: grows underground in broad-leaved woods on chalky soil; it is especially found in Beech woods.

Harvesting the fungi: from late summer to autumn. The traditional way to find truffles is to use dogs or female pigs trained to detect their scent, which is strong, sweet and pleasant. Without the use of dogs or pigs they are almost undetectable and the only chance of finding them is to know where they have been found before. Keep in mind that truffles are a rare species, so observe the foraging code.

Eating the fungi: wash and remove all traces of soil from the surface of the truffle and don't peel. Pat dry with a paper towel. Use as soon as possible after harvesting or preserve in olive oil – this has the added benefit of creating truffle-flavoured oil. Only the thinnest sliver of truffle is required to impart an incredible flavour.

Eating Truffles

• Wash and remove all traces of soil from the outside of truffles as they are used without being peeled. Use a paper towel to dry them thoroughly.
• Use as soon as possible after being harvested.
• The fungus is grated or scraped on food and into sauces and soups, just before being eaten.
• Chefs recommend that veal, chicken, fish, soufflés, pasta, rice and omelettes benefit from the addition of truffles.

Seaweeds

Seaweeds are rich in proteins and vitamins and in many places are still collected and eaten to supplement diets, especially during times of food scarcity. These plants were an important part of the diet when modern man emerged from Africa about 80,000 years ago and beach-combed his way around many parts of the world.

Unlike most land plants that reproduce through flowers and seeds, seaweed perpetuates itself through spores that develop into plants, which in turn secure themselves to mud, sand, rocks or stones by means of 'holdfasts'. These vary in size and form: those that secure stem-bases in muddy conditions often have large, spreading, root-like natures, while those found in sandy soil are bulb-like and flexible. Those that secure stems to smooth surfaces, such as rocks and stones, have holdfasts that literally glue them into position. None of these methods enable stems to extract food from their support. If they did, foundation materials such as mud or sand would eventually be eroded and fail to give support. Instead seaweeds derive their nutrients from chemicals in the water.

When harvesting seaweeds, be careful not to rip off all the fronds and leave little of the plant remaining; these species need as much consideration for rejuvenation as land plants. Freely floating pieces of seaweed can be gathered without causing damage, but if you decide to cut pieces from growing plants, do not do this close to the 'holdfast'.

Always wash fronds thoroughly before eating, since the water may be polluted with effluents piped into coastal waters. Also check that no small marine creatures remain attached to your foraged pieces of seaweed before taking it home with you. If there are, carefully remove them and put them safely back into the water.

Carrageen (*Chondrus crispus*)
Also known as: Carrageen Moss, Irish Moss, Jelly Moss, Pearl Moss

In addition to its food value, Carrageen is used as a medical tonic and a stabilizer in milk products, including ice cream. It is also ideal as a thickener in soups and as a basis for edible sausage skins. It is widely found along the northwestern and northeastern shores of the North Atlantic Ocean, especially around the coasts of Europe, including Iceland and Faroe Islands, and along the Baltic Sea.

You'll find it: in inter-tidal regions and shallow areas below low tide. It is usually attached to rocks by a stalk that varies in length.

Fronds: soft but firm and flexible and varying from greenish yellow, through red to dark purple or purplish-brown. The colour usually bleaches in strong sunlight. Fronds are up to 20 cm (8 in) long, with repeated branching that creates an impression of a fan.

Harvesting the fronds: best during mid- to late spring by removing young parts.

Using the fronds: they are very versatile and can be used fresh or dried. Wash the fronds thoroughly in running water shortly after gathering. To dry the fronds, wash then spread out on a clean surface out of doors and protect from wind-borne dirt. Repeat washing or leave in the rain. When dry, cut off tough parts and store young pieces in clean jars.

Blancmange and jelly

• To make a blancmange, use one measure of seaweed to three measures of milk, then simmer until the fronds dissolve. Sugar and flavourings can be added to suit your tastes.

• To make a jelly, use the same measures but replace the milk with water (or a mixture of water and fruit juice). Again add flavourings and colourings.

• For both jellies and blancmanges, sieve the mixture and pour into a jelly mould and allow to set. You can introduce flavourings such as ginger, vanilla, cinnamon, brandy or whisky for variety.

Bladder Wrack (*Fucus vesiculosus*)

Also known as: Black Tang, Black Tany, Bladder Fucus,
Sea Oak, Popweed, Rock Wrack and Rock Weed,

A widespread and common seaweed with branching fronds bearing conspicuous bladders that are variable in size and shape. Apart from being edible, it has been used as food for livestock and a fertilizer for soil improvement on account of its high nutrient content. Bladder Wrack is found on the shores of temperate countries bordering the North Atlantic, including Europe, Greenland, northeastern North America, and south to the Bay of Biscay.

You'll find it: along North Atlantic shores in estuaries and the middle and lower shorelines attached to rocks, timberwork and other structures. Also in sheltered areas and between high and low tides, and below inter-tidal areas where undercurrents are slight.

Fronds: The dark olive-brown, flattened branching fronds, up to 1.8 m (6 ft) long, have prominent mid-ribs with spherical air bladders peppered along them.

Harvesting the fronds: Harvest the tender young lateral branches in summer and wash thoroughly.

Using the fronds: These can be chopped and dried and added to soups, or used fresh as a thickening agent in fish, meat and vegetable dishes. It is a particularly rich source of iodine.

Knotted Wrack (*Ascophyllum nodosum*), also known as Egg Wrack, Knotted Kelp, Norwegian Kelp, is another useful seaweed to the forager. It is found in many of the same regions as Bladder Wrack. Its fronds are olive-green and can reach 1.8 m (6 ft) long, and are attached to rocks. They do not have long stalks and bear large, egg-shaped air bladders – some as large as walnuts – at regular intervals along the fronds. Cut the fronds in summer and wash under running water. It is widely used as an emulsifier in ice cream and soft drinks, in confectionery, jellies, puddings and as a thickener for soups.

Dulse (*Palmaria palmata*)
Also known as: Dillisk, Dilsk, Red Dulse, Sea Lettuce; Creathnach

Native to the shores of the North Atlantic and Baltic Sea, Dulse is a common seaweed that has been gathered as a foodstuff for centuries. It may be divided into several strap-like segments or it may appear as a single blade, and it is also variable in size and colour with red to brownish-red and purple tones.

You'll find it: attached to rocks along the middle and lower shores and extends below the lowest spring tide mark.

Fronds: The fan-like fronds, up to 30 cm (12 in) long and usually with five lobes, are tough and dark red. Sometimes, small leaflets appear at the edges of fronds with single, broad or narrow blades or strap-like segment.

Harvesting the fronds: Harvest from late spring to mid-autumn, collecting the younger, more tender fronds. Don't rip the seaweed up from its base; leave some of the fronds behind. Wash several time in clean water.

Using the fronds: rich in vitamins, minerals and trace elements, it has a high protein content. Dulse can be eaten raw or cooked in salads, stir-fries, soups and casseroles. Dulse has been mixed with mashed potato to make a kind of champ (see box). The leaves were sometimes chewed as a substitute gum. It can also be dried quite successfully, then ground and used as a flavouring.

Dulse champ
Add Dulse to creamy mashed potatoes to make a version of that great Irish staple, 'champ'.
- A couple of hours before serving, wash a good handful of Dulse in running water.
- Simmer the Dulse in a small pan of milk until tender (about 2 hours).
- Beat the cooked Dulse into hot mashed potato with a good knob of butter and season to your own taste.

Laver (*Porphyra umbilicalis*)
Also known as: Purple Laver, Red Seaweed, Stoke

Popular as a food plant, especially as a breakfast delicacy, this seaweed has a long tradition of filling stomachs. It is highly nutritious, rich in protein, carbohydrates, vitamins B, B2, A and C, plus trace elements and minerals including iodine. It is popular with vegetarians and widely sold in health shops.

Laver is native to temperate coastlines of the North Atlantic and especially around the British Isles and Ireland. It has been taken to be cultivated in other regions.

You'll find it: abundant on rocks and stones, especially in inter-tidal areas; it is highly adaptable and able to survive long periods of exposure to the air as well as being battered by wave action.

Fronds: the broad, membranous, translucent wavy-edged, irregularly shaped fronds, up to 20 cm (8 in) long, are initially green but soon become purplish-red, with a thin but strong, polythene-like texture.

Harvesting the fronds: cut during spring and summer and wash in clean water several times.

Using the fronds: fresh fronds make an excellent wrapper when baking fish. To cook, repeat the washing then boil in only a small amount of water, until soft and with the appearance of a very dark, spinach-like purée. This purée is then coated in oatmeal and fried and eaten with bacon and eggs, although small boiled potatoes and knobs of butter are another choice. It also goes well in sandwiches, and chopped in salads. The purée can also be stored in sterilized jars, which can then be stored in the refridgerator for a short time.

Laverbread The Welsh make this seaweed into laverbread by boiling the seaweed for several hours, then puréeing and drying the results. It is sold either as it is or rolled in oatmeal then eaten with bacon which is considered to be a great treat. It also accompanies lamb, crab, monkfish and cockles extremely well and can also be made into soup.

Oarweed (*Laminaria digitata*)

Also known as: Common Kelp, Fingered Tangle,
Horsetail Kelp, Kelp, Sea Tangle, Tangle, Kombu

A widespread seaweed that has been used as a source of human food as
well as to feed livestock in times of hardship, Oarweed is native to the
temperate coastlines of the North Atlantic Ocean of both Europe and
North America.

You'll find it: close to the low-water line, where it is regularly covered
by water. It also grows well in shallow pools and can soon colonize large
areas, anchoring itself to rocks and pebbles with a claw-like holdfast.
Fronds: brown, usually about 1.5 m (5 ft) long and with finger-like
branches. Occasionally, when in large and undisturbed colonies, it is
claimed to grow 3 m (10 ft) or more long.
Harvesting the fronds: cut during spring and early summer to use
fresh. Alternatively, they can be harvested and dried in the open in an
area sheltered from wind-blown dust. When dry, place in clean jars and
put in the refrigerator.
Eating the fronds: young stems can be eaten fresh (first wash in running
water), and are said to resemble the flavour of peanuts. Additionally,
they can be made into a flour, as well as being added to dishes that
contain lentils, vegetables and rice. Alternatively, they can be washed,
shredded and pickled as a condiment.

Bean softener Along with other
kelps, Oarweed is a traditional
constituent of bean-based stews in
Japan. It is supposed to speed up the
cooking time by softening the beans
and adding thickness to the stew.
When using kelp in this way, put a
few strips of dried kelp in the base
of a pan, then add the beans and
simmer gently until they are tender.

Gutweed (*Enteromorpha intestinalis*)

Sometimes known as: Grass Kelp, Sea Grass,
Hollow Green Seaweed

Widespread throughout the world, Gutweed is
also botanically known as *Ulva intestinalis* and looks
amazingly like ropes of intestines.

You will find it: one of the most adaptable seaweeds,
flourishing in rocky pools, and brackish water where there is fresh
water running through it, as well as on rocks, mud and sand.
Fronds: The green, unbranched, tubular, inflated fronds are up to
30 cm (12 in) long. It is an annual and sometimes pieces become
detached and float to the surface, where they survive in a floating mass.
By the end of summer the fronds become bleached by the sun.
Harvesting and using the fronds: Gather it in spring or early
summer, when it is best stir-fried until crisp.

Sea Lettuce (*Ulva lactuca*)

A cosmopolitan seaweed, it is found on the shores
of Europe, west and east coasts of North America,
Central America, South America, Caribbean
islands, Indian Ocean islands, southwest Asia,
Pacific islands, Australia and New Zealand.

You will find it: attached to rocks, either between the
tidal area or slightly below.
Fronds: tough crumple-edged green to dark green nearly
translucent fronds 18 cm (7 in) long and 30 cm (12 in) across.
Gathering the fronds: The leaves are much prized and
gathered in early spring or summer.
Eating the fronds: wash thoroughly, chop up and served raw in salads.
They are also added to soups and are a central part of some Japanese
dishes. They also make a great wrap for baked fish.

Shellfish

Shellfish, like seaweeds, have been gathered by humans from beaches and rocks for thousands and thousands of years. Early people would not have realized the benefits of a seafood-rich diet and just considered them to be 'stomach fillers', but for us the benefits are clear. Shellfish are high in protein but low in saturated fats, so help reduce the risk of heart disease, decrease blood pressure and lower blood fats.

They offer an exciting change in diet for the coastal forager, although care needs to be taken to ensure that all shellfish is clear of contamination from effluents discharged into the sea. Always wash any shellfish thoroughly before eating and ensure they are still alive. Dead shellfish are extremely dangerous to eat and may result in a very unpleasant illness and perhaps a hospital visit.

Killing shellfish humanely presents welfare problems. Dropping them live into saucepans of boiling water is cruel, and although it is the traditional way to kill them, it need not be the method of choice today. Lobsters, crayfish and crabs earlier killed by plunging into boiling water are now dispatched more humanely by stunning them electrically. It is fast and efficient, reduces harmful bacteria and improves their texture and taste. In a fraction of a second the electrical charge knocks them unconscious and by sustaining the current, quickly destroys their entire nervous system. Compare this to the three minutes or more it takes for a lobster to die when in it is immersed in boiling water!

These electrical stunners are readily available and their use is recommended by many animal welfare organizations. The shellfish described in this chapter are much smaller than lobsters, crabs and crayfish and, unfortunately, at present there is no electrical stunner available that will kill them. Therefore, after cleaning them, place in a freezer prior to dropping in boiling water – this puts them into a dormant state, which alleviates some welfare concerns.

Clam (*Mya arenaria*)

Also known as: Long-necked Clam, Long Necks, Nannynose, Piss Clams, Sand Gaper, Soft Clam, Soft-shelled Clam, Soft Shells, Steamers

A popular seashore delicacy, a clam has a hinged oval, soft white to pale-grey or brownish shell up to 13 cm (5 in) across. It buries itself 15–25 cm (6–10 in) deep in mud, and extends two long, fused siphons to the surface of the mud to draw in seawater that is filtered for food and then expelled. Clams are found along European North Atlantic coast lines and also along the eastern coasts of North America.

You'll find them: usually on the middle and lower shorelines, in brackish water and along estuaries. They prefer a sandy-mud base with some gravel.

Harvesting clams: if pressure is applied to the surface of the area where clams are thought to be, they often eject water from their siphon tips. Dig them up carefully and place in a deep bucket of seawater for a few days so that they clean themselves.

End their lives humanely (see page 115) before scalding in boiling water for 15 minutes. Trim off the siphons.

Eating clams: can be steamed whole in their shells, or the flesh removed and fried, baked or boiled and served with a sauce. They are delicious with pasta – *Spaghetti alle vongole* is a great Italian favourite.

Clam chowder

- Scrub 16–20 clams and place in a pan with a bit of water. Cover and cook until the clams open. Discard any that don't open. Take off the heat. Reserve the juice.
- Fry 3–4 rashers of bacon with a chopped onion until cooked.
- Cube 4 medium potatoes and place in a separate pot with 420 ml (14 fl oz) milk, a bay leaf and a good pinch of salt and pepper. Cook until just tender.
- Add the bacon and onions, the clams taken from their shells and reserved clam juice to the pan and heat through for five minutes.
- Check the seasoning, crush some of the potatoes with a fork and serve garnished with chopped parsley.

Cockle (*Cerastoderma edule*)
Also known as: Common Cockle

A popular seafood, with a ribbed shell up to
6 cm (2½ in) wide and variable in colour;
cream, light-yellow or pale brown, cockles
are found around the eastern coastlines of
the North Atlantic Ocean, from west Africa to
Norway, and along North Sea coasts.

You'll find them: most abundant on tidal flats,
in bays and estuaries, and usually in sandy mud,
sand or fine gravel.
Harvesting cockles: they are found most often
after the tide has gone out and usually in clusters.
They are up to 7.5 cm (3 in) below the surface, so
use your hands to reveal them. Do not gather small
ones – anything under 2.5 cm (1 in) wide. Wash off any
mud and sand and carefully place them in a bucket of seawater; leave
alone for a day or so until they clean themselves, then put in a bucket of
fresh clean water for a few hours to remove the taste of salt.
Eating cockles: to end their lives, use the most humane method
available (see page 115) before scalding them in boiling water. First,
however, check that they are alive by prising open the shell. With their
shells open, cockles cook in boiling water within five minutes. They are
eaten in many ways, from cooking with bacon, to being made into soups
or pies. Cockles are often eaten simply steamed with a shallot vinegar for
added zip. Like other forms of seafood, they
lend themselves to pasta and rice dishes
including risottos, paellas
and also as an ingredient
in fish soups and stews.

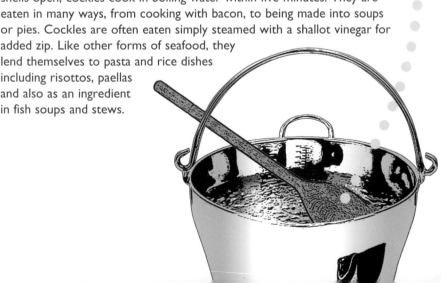

Common Limpet (*Patella vulgata*)
Also known as: European Limpet

A well-known seafood with a conical, greyish-white shell up to 6 cm
(2½ in) across; those on the lower shoreline have lower shells than ones
higher up. Limpets move by means of a muscular 'foot', which is yellow,
orange or brown with a green or greyish tint. They graze on algae and
seek a resting place when the tide retreats.

  This limpet is widely seen on coastlines along the North Atlantic,
from the Arctic Circle to Portugal in the south. It has been foraged for
centuries as a welcome source of protein.

You'll find them: attached to
rocks and stones from the high- to
low-water levels, and also under
water.

Harvesting limpets: choose large
specimens from rocks that are washed
daily by tides and use a strong knife to
prize them from their holding positions.
Wash and place in a bucket of seawater for
a day or so. Then, put in clean water for a few
hours to remove the taste of salt.

  To end their lives, use the most humane method available (see page
115) before dropping into boiling water for five or so minutes.

Eating limpets: limpet soup is popular, as well as 'dressing' large ones
and frying them in a little butter, pepper and vinegar. Small limpets are
best boiled.

Common Mussel (*Mytilus edulis*)

Also known as: Bay
Mussel, Blue Mussel,
Edible Mussel

Perhaps one of the
best-known edible shellfish,
Common Mussels grow up to
10 cm (4 in) long, with purple,
blue or occasionally brown and bright
green smooth shells showing concentric growth lines.

Widely found in coastal areas of the North Atlantic, along the shores
of North America and Europe, and in other polar and temperate waters
around the world.

You'll find them: between areas of high and low tide, attached to rocks
and other hard marine surfaces. They secure themselves in position by
thread-like structures that grow from the foot of the mussel.

Mussels in a parcel

- Clean and prepare 1 kg (2¼ lb) mussels and preheat oven to 220°C (425°F/gas mark 7).
- Finely chop 2 cloves garlic, a handful of parsley and a small chilli.
- To make parcels, tear off two large pieces of greaseproof paper and pile the mussels (divided into two) onto the paper.
- Sprinkle parsley, garlic and chilli over the piles. Drizzle over a little olive oil, a squeeze of lemon, season with black pepper and tie the parcels.
- Place on a baking sheet and bake in oven for 5–8 minutes, then serve.

Harvesting mussels: gather and put in
a bucket of clean water overnight, then
change the water and leave for a further
day to remove the salt.
To avoid food poisoning, pick only those
from clean, shingle or stony beaches, away
from effluent out-flows. Before cooking,
check that the mussel is alive; discard any
with cracked or gapping shells. Never eat
dead mussels; those suitable for eating
have tightly closed shells or ones that
snap shut when tapped.

Eating mussels: can be steamed,
baked or fried, taking care not to
overcook as they then become tough.
Popular in pasta dishes, seafood soups,
fish stews such as bouillabaisse, and
Spanish dishes such as paella.

Common Winkle (*Littorina littorea*)

Also known as: Common Periwinkle, Edible Periwinkle, Winkle

This small, edible shellfish is usually about 12 mm (½ in) high at maturity but occasionally 30 mm (1¼ in). It has a dark grey or black conical shell that becomes smooth with age.

It is native to coastal areas of the northeastern North Atlantic, from northern Spain to Scandinavia and Russia. It has also been introduced to the Atlantic coast of North America.

You'll find them: native to a large area, from the upper shoreline down to the water's edge; also, on mudflats and in estuaries.

Harvesting winkles: place them in a bucket of clean water overnight to free them from sand and grit.

Eating winkles: end their lives using the most humane method available (see page 115).They are cooked by gently simmering for about ten minutes. Their meat is high in protein but low in fat, and needs 'winkling' out of their shells with a pin.

Like cockles, they were and are traditionally sold from seafood stalls in pint jugs accompanied by a sharp vinegar dressing and eaten on the street.

Eating winkles

Winkles used to be an essential part of the diet in countries where these useful little creatures were harvested. Nowadays, there are few recipes for winkles, although they have been cooked in omelettes, used in fishy stews and served with mustard, lemon and garlic. You might try your foraged and steamed winkles dipped in a garlicy mayonnaise, or make them into a sandwich with some watercress, a good grinding of pepper and a squeeze of lemon.

Oyster (*Ostrea edulis*)

Also known as: Colchester Native Oyster, European
Flat Oyster, Mud Oyster

Nowadays, oysters are difficult to find because
they have been excessively harvested in earlier
years. However, they are worth seeking out.
There are numerous kinds of oyster but
generally are oval or pear-shaped, with a rough
and scaly surface, off-white, yellowish or cream
in colour with light brown or bluish concentric
bands. Sizes vary, usually to 10 cm (4 in) long.
   Oyster is native to western European
coastlines, from Morocco in the south to
Spitsbergen in Norway. They are found widely
around the world, and have been an important
addition to human diets for millennia. These days,
oysters are intensively farmed
and the market for them is prodigious.

Grilled oysters

• Steam open 12 oysters in a large
pot and replace oysters on the
flattened half of the shell.
• Mash together a good knob of
butter, chopped garlic and parsley
and about 3 tablespoons toasted
breadcrumbs.
• Dot each oyster with a bit of the
herby butter.
• Season with salt and pepper.
• Half-fill a roasting pan with rock
salt and wedge the oysters onto the
salt to keep them upright.
• Place under a hot grill for 2–3
minutes until the tops are lightly
browned and then eat immediately.

You'll find them: in shallow coastal
water with firm mud, rocks, muddy
sand or gravel bases.
Harvesting and eating oysters:
usually eaten raw, with lemon and
Tabasco sauce. Be alert to
contamination as a result
of pollution.

Glossary

Annual A plant that germinates from seed, grows and flowers within a single year.

Anther The pollen-bearing male part of a flower. A small stem, called a filament, supports the anther. Collectively, anthers are known as stamen.

Axil The junction between a leaf and stem, from where side shoots or flowers may develop.

Basal leaves These grow around the bases of plants and sometimes differ in size and shape from the ones that appear higher up and attached to the stem.

Berry A fleshy or succulent fruit with small seeds, such as currants, grapes, gooseberries and tomatoes.

Biennial A plant that takes two seasons to complete its life-cycle and to produce seeds. In the first year seeds are sown, they germinate, grow and produce plants. In the second year, the same plant produces flowers, seeds and then dies.

Blanching The exclusion of light from the stems of some vegetables to whiten them and improve their flavour.

Bletted A process used with certain fleshy fruits, when they are allowed to ripen to a point at which they start to decay and ferment. The Medlar (*Mespilus germanica*) is an example where the fruits are allowed to become bletted before being eaten.

Bud A tightly-packed and closed immature shoot or flower.

Bulb A swollen, underground, food-storage organ with a bud-like structure. It is formed of fleshy scales attached to a flattened stem called a basal plate.

Bulbils Small, immature bulbs found around the bases of some bulbs. They can be detached, sown and encouraged to form roots. Some leaves produce bulbils.

Bracket fungi Type of fungi with a shelf-like fruiting body that grows on tree trunks and other surfaces, rather than growing in soil at ground-level.

Calyx The outer ring of a flower, usually green, which protects the flower when it is in bud.

Catkin A dense, unisexual flowering arrangement. Those on hazels are pendulous, but with willows they are erect.

Cladode A flattened, leaf-like stem.

Clove A segment of a bulb; frequently used to refer to a small part of a garlic bulb. May also refer to a dried flower bud of the tropical tree *Eugenia caryophyllus*, which is used whole or ground into a spice.

Conifer Plants with a tree- or shrub-like nature that bear cones, such as with pines, firs and spruces. Some conifers are evergreen, while others, such as larches, are deciduous.

Corm An underground storage organ formed of a stem base greatly swollen laterally.

Cultivar A plant raised in cultivation, rather than appearing naturally and without any interference from man. Properly, the vast majority of plants known as varieties should be called cultivars, but the term 'variety' is better-known and often seen in books, as well as used in general conversation.

Deciduous A plant that sheds its leaves at the beginning of its dormant season and produces a fresh set during the following year, at the beginning of its growing period. This usually applies to trees, shrubs and some conifers.

Dormant Resting period in a plant's life, normally in late autumn and winter in temperate regions, when a plant makes no noticeable growth.

Escapee A plant grown in cultivation that, having escaped into the wild, establishes itself in the countryside.

Evergreen A plant that continuously sheds and grows fresh leaves throughout the year; therefore, it always appears to be green. Some shrubs, trees and conifers are evergreen.

Fines herbes French term for finely chopped herbs. They are used fresh or dried, as seasonings and to flavour sauces.

Flora A book containing information about native plants in a particular region or country. Also used to denote plants in general.

Floret Usually very small flowers and part of a larger inflorescence.

Flower Specialized part of a seed-bearing plant and concerned with reproduction.

Genus A group of plants with similar botanical characteristics. Some genera contain many species, others just one (they are known as monotypic).

Germination The process that occurs within a seed when given adequate moisture, air and warmth. The coat of the seed ruptures and a seed leaf (or leaves) grows up towards the light. A root develops at the same time.

Green manuring The growing of a crop, such as White mustard, that can be subsequently dug into the soil to improve its physical and nutritional qualities.

Herbaceous A plant that dies down to soil level after the completion of each season's growth, usually in autumn or early winter. During spring of the following year, the plant develops fresh growth.

Herbal A book containing information about medicinal and culinary herbs, their uses and properties.

Inflorescence The part of a plant which bears the flowers.

Lateral A side-shoot growing from a main stem of a tree or shrub.

Linear leaves Narrow and often long.

Lobed leaves Having round projections, around their edges or at the top.

Mast The fruit of trees such as beech, oak and Sweet Chestnut.

Naturalized A plant that has been introduced into another country or area and has established itself as one of the population.

Perennial Usually used to describe herbaceous plants, but it also applies to any plant that lives for several years, including shrubs, trees and climbers.

Rhizome Horizontal, creeping, underground or partly underground stem that acts as a storage organ. Some can be slender, others are fleshy and thick.

Runner A shoot that grows along the ground, at intervals rooting into the soil.

Saprophytic A plant that lives on decaying organic material.

Shrub A woody perennial with stems growing from soil-level and without a trunk. Some plants grow as either shrubs or trees.

Species A group of plants that breed together and have the same characteristics.

Stamen The male part of a flower, formed of the anthers and filaments.

Stigma The female part of a flower on which pollen alights.

Stipe The stalk (stem) that bears the fruiting, spore-bearing part of a mushroom. It can also apply to the leaf-stalks on ferns.

Succulent Usually applied to thick and fleshy leaves and stems. It can also refer to a group of plants with succulent features.

Style Female part of a flower – the stalk that joins the stigma to the ovary.

Tap-root A long, strong, primary root on some plants, often penetrating deep into the soil.

Tree A woody plant with a single main stem (trunk).

Tuber A thickened, fleshy root or stem, wholly or partly under the soil's surface.

Variety Naturally occurring variation within a species. At one time, all variations within a species were known as varieties. Now, correctly, varieties raised in cultivation are called cultivars.

Further reading

Wayside Kitchen Herbs
Culinary and medicinal herbs, HMS
Stationery Office, London

General Food Books
Guide to Edible Plants and Animals,
A. D. Livingston, Helen Livingston,
Wordsworth Editions Ltd., Herts
The Oxford Book of Food Plants,
G. B. Masefield, M. Wallis, S. G.
Harrison, B. E. Nicholson, OUP

Wild Fruits, Nuts and Fungi
Wild Fruits and Nuts, Geoffrey Eley,
EP Publishing Ltd., West Yorkshire
Mushrooms and other Fungi of Britain
and Northern Europe, Geoffrey Kibby,
Dragon's World Ltd., Surrey
Mushrooms and Toadstools, Stefan Buczacki,
Collins Gem, HarperCollins, London
Collins Guide to Mushrooms and Toadstools
of Britain and Europe, Stefan Buczacki,
HarperCollins, London
Field Guide to Mushrooms of Britain and
Europe, Helmut and Renate Grnert, The
Crowood Press Ltd., Wiltshire

European Native Plants
British Wild Flowers, John Hutchinson,
Penguin Books Ltd., Middlesex
Flora of the British Isles, A. R. Clapham,
T. G. Tutin, E. F. Warburg, CU
The Englishman's Flora, Geoffrey Grigson,
Helicon Publishing Ltd., Oxford

Trees, Keith Rushforth, Mitchell Beazley
Ltd., London
Trees and Bushes of Britain and Europe, Oleg
Polunin, Granada Publishing Ltd., London
Trees of Britain and Northern Europe, Alan
Mitchell, William Collins, Sons & Co.
Ltd., London
Wild Flowers of Britain and Northern Europe,
Richard Fitter, Alastair Fitter, Marjorie
Blamey, William Collins Sons & Co. Ltd.,
London
Wayside and Woodland Blossoms, Edward
Step, Frederick Warne & Co. Ltd.,
London
Wayside and Woodland Trees, Edward Step,
Frederick Warne & Co. Ltd., London

North American Native Plants
Field Book of American Trees and Shrubs,
F. Schuyler Mathews, G. P. Putnam's
Sons, New York and London
Field Book of American Wild Flowers,
F. Schuyler Mathews , G. P. Putnam's
Sons, New York and London
Field Book of Western Wild Flowers, Margaret
Armstrong , G. P. Putnam's Sons, New
York and London
Hortus Third – A Concise Dictionary of Plants
Cultivated in the United States and Canada,
Macmillan Publishing Co., Inc., New York
Native Trees of Canada, Department of
Resources and Development, Forestry
Branch, Ottawa
A Guide to Field Identification of Trees of
North America, C. Frank Brockman,
Golden Press, New York